FH

CULTURE SMART!

IRAN

Stuart Williams

·K·U·P·E·R·A·R·D·

ISBN 978 1 85733 847 8
This book is also available as an e-book: eISBN 978 1 85733 849 2

British Library Cataloguing in Publication Data
A CIP catalogue entry for this book is available from the British Library

First published in Great Britain
by Kuperard, an imprint of Bravo Ltd
59 Hutton Grove, London N12 8DS
Tel: +44 (0) 20 8446 2440 Fax: +44 (0) 20 8446 2441
www.culturesmart.co.uk
Inquiries: sales@kuperard.co.uk

Series Editor Geoffrey Chesler
Design Bobby Birchall

Printed in Malaysia

About the Author

STUART WILLIAMS is a British journalist specializing in the Middle East, Russia, and Turkey. A graduate in German and Russian from Worcester College, Oxford, he has worked for international news agency Agence France-Presse (AFP) in several countries, including long-term postings living in Iran, Russia, and Turkey, covering protests, conflict, and post-imperial societies. Stuart first traveled around Iran as a tourist after leaving university and was immediately entranced by a country that appeared so different from its image abroad. He worked for two full years in Tehran as one of very few foreign reporters based inside Iran, an experience that did not diminish his enthusiasm. He is now based in Istanbul.

The Culture Smart! series is continuing to expand.
For further information and latest titles visit
www.culturesmart.co.uk

The publishers would like to thank **CultureSmart!**Consulting for its help in researching and developing the concept for this series.

CultureSmart!Consulting creates tailor-made seminars and consultancy programs to meet a wide range of corporate, public-sector, and individual needs. Whether delivering courses on multicultural team building in the USA, preparing Chinese engineers for a posting in Europe, training call-center staff in India, or raising the awareness of police forces to the needs of diverse ethnic communities, it provides essential, practical, and powerful skills worldwide to an increasingly international workforce.

For details, visit www.culturesmartconsulting.com

CultureSmart!Consulting and **CultureSmart!** guides have both contributed to and featured regularly in the weekly travel program "Fast Track" on BBC World TV.

contents

contents

Note: The book uses the conventional English transliterations for Persian names, e.g. Hossein rather than Hussein (but the Arabic form for Saddam Hussein), Mohammad rather than Mohammed, etc.

Map of Iran

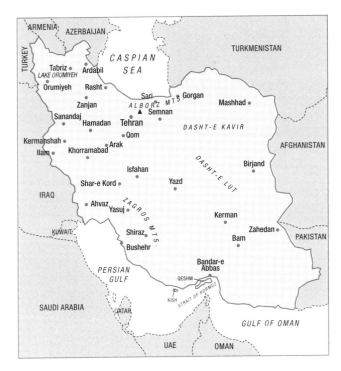

introduction

Iran—the very name shimmers with mystique and allure, but also a sense of inaccessibility and isolation. Iran, however, is now opening up to visitors and business as never before in recent years, making visiting this country with its thousands of years of heritage and traditions, unique in the Middle East, not just tempting but also realistic.

For centuries, foreigners have been entranced and seduced by this land. Iran's best-known export—the Persian carpet—has always attracted buyers for its whiff of mystique. Travelers have been drawn in by the echoes of the extraordinary ancient history contained in the word "Persia."

Beyond the clichés and the stereotypes, what is the real Iran like at the start of the twenty-first century? For sure, the country still offers romance and the exotic. It is a place where people sing medieval poetry on mountaintops. Where the bread is never more delicious than when it is baked early in the morning. Where the intricate patterns of Islamic art thrill visitors of whatever religion.

But Iran is also a modern society that is experiencing great change. It is still feeling the effects of the Islamic Revolution of 1979—a true revolution in the sense that it completely changed the country's political orientation within days. The Revolution imposed strict rules on social behavior, and all women must cover themselves, alcohol is prohibited, and the mixing of unrelated couples is banned. But the image of a reactionary, strict society only goes part of the way. Social restrictions have loosened considerably in the last years. Today strict Islamic rules coexist with an increasingly dynamic society being driven by an overwhelmingly young population. The 2015 deal ending the years-long and explosive standoff over the Iranian nuclear program raises the prospect of a new chapter in Iran's relations with the West as sanctions that had hit all areas of the economy are finally dismantled. The US, which went from being a close ally of the Shah to the arch enemy of the Islamic Republic, now seems slightly less the "Great Satan" in Tehran.

This book aims to show how life in Iran really is and how visitors can feel comfortable in its society. It explains the basic culture of a country full of surprises. Despite Iran's deep commitment to Islam, the pre-Islamic Zoroastrian past is still part of everyday life. Its language, Persian, shares the same linguistic roots as English or French. It is a country where a nominally democratic parliamentary system is overlaid by an unelected theocracy. And where "no thank you" really does sometimes mean "yes please."

The only way to break through the stereotypes is to experience Iranian culture firsthand. "*Iran keshvar-e jadouyi-e*" ("Iran is a magical country") is how many Iranians sum up this entrancing, beautiful, and sometimes infuriating place. If nothing else, it is a land whose inhabitants genuinely wish visitors "*Khosh amadi*!"—"Welcome!"

Key Facts

Official Name	The Islamic Republic of Iran (*Jomhouri-ye Eslami-ye Iran*)	Iran became an Islamic Republic after the 1979 Islamic Revolution that toppled the US-backed shah.
Capital City	Tehran	Pop. more than 8 million; at least 13 million incl. suburbs and satellite cities
Main Cities	Iran's second city is the holy city of Mashhad (pop. 3 million).	Other big cities include Tabriz, Isfahan, and Shiraz.
Population	Around 80 million. Population growth is 1.3%.	68.5% live in urban areas, compared with around 22% in 1940.
Area	636,296 sq. miles (1,648,000 sq. km)	The highest point is Mount Damavand, at 18,606 ft (5,671 m).
Climate	Hugely varied. The Caspian Sea region has up to 78.74 inches (2,000 mm) of rain a year, while the interior desert areas are dry almost all year. The north has freezing winters; temp. on the Persian Gulf can reach a sticky 104°F (40°C) in summer.	The wettest main city is Rasht, the driest is Yazd. The hottest is the coastal city of Bandar Abbas, and the coldest is the northern city of Ardebil.
Language	The main language is Persian (Farsi), written using the Arabic alphabet with slight modifications.	Minority languages include Azeri, Kurdish, Arabic, and Armenian.

Religion	The state religion is Islam. The overwhelming majority of Iranians adhere to the Shiite branch. A minority of Iranians are Sunnis.	Other recognized minority religions are Christianity, Judaism, and Zoroastrianism. The Bahai faith is not recognized.
Government	Since the Islamic Revolution a mix of theocracy and democracy. The top political figure is the Supreme Leader, a cleric. Under him are a president and a parliament.	Elections held every four years for the president and the parliament. The Supreme Leader is chosen and supervised by a clerical body elected by the people.
Dress Code	Women must wear the Islamic headscarf and cover all bodily contours in public. Men should not wear shorts, except when playing organized sports.	
Currency	The rial (IRR): 1 rial=100 dinars. 30,000 rials are worth around US $1.	Transactions are often carried out in tomans (1 toman=10 rials).
Media	Television is state-run. Several channels available in most cities. Satellite TV is banned but widely watched in Tehran and other cities.	Lively Persian-language press scene but newspapers subject to strict controls and liberal publications have frequently been banned.
Electricity	220 volts, 50 Hz	2-pronged plugs
Internet Domain	.ir	
Telephone	Iran's country code is 98.	To dial abroad out of Iran, dial 00.
Time Zone	GMT + 3.5 hours in winter, GMT + 4.5 hours in summer	Daylight saving time was restored in summer 2008.

chapter one

LAND &
PEOPLE

GEOGRAPHY AND CLIMATE

Straddling the frontiers of Europe and South and
Central Asia, Iran encompasses a huge diversity of
cultures and landscapes. It has western borders with
Turkey, possibly a future European Union member.
To the northwest lie the former Soviet republics
of Armenia and Azerbaijan. There is a northern
border with the reclusive former Soviet republic of
Turkmenistan and then the Caspian Sea, a major
economic asset. When the Soviet Union collapsed
in the 1990s, Iran found the number of its northern
neighbors had tripled.

To the west, its neighbor is one-time foe and
now close ally Iraq. Further south are the sultry
waters of the Persian Gulf, across which lies the
Arabian Peninsula. To the east, Iran borders desert
regions of Pakistan and further north conflict-torn
Afghanistan.

As a result of this extraordinary geographic
position, it is sometimes hard to define Iranian
culture. On occasion it appears very eastern
and even mystical, while at others historic links
to Europe and the West are more evident than
elsewhere in the region. Regional influences and
minority groups have also left substantial traces.

Climate

Iran's weather is one of its greatest assets, and it is sorely missed by the millions who now live in the diaspora. Iranians will proudly tell you how it is possible on the same day to be sweltering by the Persian Gulf while a friend is battling below freezing temperatures climbing a mountain in the north. The weather varies greatly from region to region throughout the year. "*Iran chahar fasl-e!*" ("Iran has four seasons!") is a proud and often-repeated refrain. And it is true, the weather is spectacular: normally sunny, with short but intense periods of rain or snow.

The capital Tehran has the full kaleidoscope of weather—heavy snowfalls in the winter (starting in December) usually cause chaos in the city center but delight skiing fans who flock to several resorts within a short drive north of the city.

Spring breaks around March with occasional but heavy showers. True summer starts in May, with temperatures kept bearable in Tehran and several other cities by their high altitude. Fall is a long and beautiful season in the capital with stable, sunny weather often lasting into November. In the winter months temperatures can plunge to -4°F (-20°C) in the north of Iran, and even in central Tehran prolonged periods below freezing are common. By contrast, the temperature in Tehran can rise over 86°F (30°C) in summer; on the humid littoral cities of the Persian Gulf temperatures in excess of 104°F (40°C) are common in summer.

Landscape

The landscape of Iran is of breathtaking diversity. The northern provinces bordering the Caspian Sea are relatively lush areas with high precipitation that burst into bloom in springtime. In contrast two deserts make up around one-third of the country. The massive Dasht-e Kavir that starts east of Tehran and the Dasht-e Lut that heads toward the Pakistan border are areas with sand dunes and endless scrubland that may seem more familiar in Arab and African countries. As well as these deserts, there are also great mountain ranges. The Alborz Mountains that rise high above Tehran include Iran's highest peak, Mount Damavand, an extinct volcano rising to 18,606 feet (5,671 m), whose huge cone is one of the country's iconic images. Extending down the country's western edge like a massive spine is the long Zagros range, the other main chain of mountains.

Iran has a huge interior lake in its north, Lake Orumiyeh. On the Persian Gulf, Kish and Qeshm islands are being heavily promoted by the authorities as tourist destinations.

POPULATION

Iran's majority population is Persian (*Fars*), who still proudly see themselves as the descendants of the great Achaemenian empire that ruled Iran and much of the region between 550 and 330 BCE. They speak Persian (Farsi), a language of Indo-European origin (see more in Chapter 9). Persians adhere to the Shiite branch of Islam.

The population is some 80 million. There has been drastic population growth and a move from villages to towns over the last half century, transforming the social makeup and population density.

Ethnic and Religious Minorities

Iran is also home to several ethnic minorities, reflecting its position between a number of cultures. The largest minority are ethnic Azeris (*Azari*, though often referred to by all Iranians as Turks), a Turkic people who have substantial populations especially in the north and northwestern provinces as well as Tehran. The Azeri population in Iran is substantially larger than that in the neighboring state of Azerbaijan itself. Speaking a Turkic language, the Azeris also adhere to Shiite Islam and are generally very well integrated into society.

There are also substantial Kurdish populations in the western provinces, with their own distinctive culture and clothing (baggy trousers for men and colorful head scarves for women). They are generally Sunni Muslims.

Concentrated in the western Khuzestan province is an Arab population consisting of a mixture of Sunnis and Shiites. The Sunni Baluch form a large population in the Sistan-Baluchestan province that borders Pakistan and Afghanistan. Other important ethnic minorities include the Turkmen. There is also a substantial nomad population in Iran, although the numbers living a truly nomadic life have dropped sharply since campaigns to settle them in the 1920s and 1930s.

Few people outside Iran are aware that religious minorities exist within its strict Islamic system. The Islamic Republic's constitution recognizes and guarantees the right to freedom of worship for Christians, Jews, and Zoroastrians. All these groups have their own members of parliament and their own cultural centers. It is, however, strictly forbidden for Muslims to convert to other religions.

The largest Christian community is the Armenians (*Aramaneh*), a group who have lived in the territory of Iran for centuries. Despite numbering only around fifty thousand, they are prominent in professional trades and their churches are easy to spot in major centers like Tehran, Isfahan, and Tabriz. Visitors will also see shop signs in the unique Armenian script in their quarters. There are also smaller populations of Assyrian and Chaldean Christians.

Iran's Jewish (*Yahudi*, or *Kalimi* for specifically Iranian Jews) population is the largest in the Middle East outside Israel. However, the current number of around twenty thousand is well below the approximately one hundred thousand from before the Revolution. Although former president Mahmoud Ahmadinejad and other officials have launched virulent tirades against Israel, the authorities insist that their only objection is to Zionism, and that Iranian Jews have full rights and freedoms. Jews in Iran are often prominent and successful in the bazaar trade. The Islamic Republic has always refused to recognize Israel, which was a close ally of the pro-US imperial Iranian regime.

Zoroastrians (*Zartoshti*) adhere to the religion that was dominant in Iran before the Arab invasion in the seventh century. Contrary to popular belief, Zoroastrians are not fire worshipers, although fire appears in their rituals and temples symbolizing life, growth, and purity. There are tens of thousands of Zoroastrians in Iran, although again numbers have been hit by emigration.

Iran's biggest minority before the Islamic revolution were the Bahais, who advocate the unity of all religions. However, the Islamic authorities deem Bahais to be apostates and the group is not recognized by the constitution as a religious minority. Bahais have none of the rights enjoyed by other minorities and those remaining are forced to pursue their faith underground.

A BRIEF HISTORY

Iranians are proud of their history and still see themselves as the direct descendants of the Persians who built one of the greatest empires in world history 2,500 years ago.

The name "Iran," which is now applied to the modern, ethnically diverse country, has ancient roots, coming from the word "Aryan," in reference to the Indo-Europeans who entered the country in around 1000 BCE. Iran was for long called "Persia" (*Fars*) in the West, although strictly speaking this is a rendering of the name of the southern Iranian province of Fars (which is still known as such) from where the Achaemenian Iranian kings ruled.

The country also witnessed, just over three decades ago, one of the most important events of modern times, the Islamic Revolution of 1979 that ousted the pro-US shah, Mohammad Reza Pahlavi, and ended 2,500 years of monarchy in Iran.

Early Times

Pottery dating from 5,000 BCE is evidence of a lively early culture in Iran. There are also indications of urban societies forming as early as around 3000 BCE, such as Tepe Yahya, an archaeological site in the eastern Kerman province. By 2,000 BCE civilization appears to have been flourishing in Iran, as shown by the impressively elaborate bronze and copper work found at Tepe Yahya and Shahdad in the same region.

A growing civilization was meanwhile developing in southwest Iran, around the modern Khuzestan province on the border with Iraq, in the region known as Elam. It was in Elam that one of the first great cities of Iran, Susa (*Shoush* in Persian), was built, a capital that would later be expanded by the great Achaemenian kings. The sophistication of their culture is shown by the clay tablets in a proto-Elamite script that have been found in the area as well as accomplished metalwork. It was in the Elamite period that the great ziggurat temple of Choqa Zanbil was built, the remains of which still stand today—it is the best-preserved such site in the region. Elamite civilization appears to have reached a high point around 1500–1100 BCE, but was badly hit by the invasion of the famous Babylonian king Nebuchadnezzar at the end of the twelfth century BCE. But archaeologists have found increasingly sophisticated and innovative examples of bronze work and pottery from the years 1100 to 500 BCE.

[handwritten margin notes: Elamite 1500 – 1100 BCE; invaded by Nebuchadnezzar in 12th C BCE]

Many of the great treasures of this and other periods of ancient Iranian history are to be found in Europe, rather than Iran. For example, a large number of the objects excavated at Susa are now in the Louvre in Paris. Looting and colonial rule in the nineteenth and early twentieth centuries mean that many

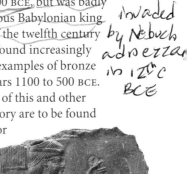

treasures from Elamite, Achaemenian, and Sasanian Iran are held in Paris and London, something that still rankles modern Iranians. The famous Cyrus Cylinder from the sixth century BCE —said to be the world's first declaration of human rights—is held in the British Museum. Its historic four-month loan to the National Museum in Tehran in 2010 caused a sensation in the city.

Achaemenian Kings : 550 - 330 BCE

The Persian Empire

The Achaemenian kings who ruled from 550 to 330 BCE are the most famous rulers of ancient Iran. They built a great empire that at its height stretched from Libya to India and remains a source of great pride for Iranians today.

Medes

By 600 BCE a people known as the Medes had won control of an area around their main city of Ecbatana, the site of the modern city of Hamedan. They even

then

Cyrus the Great

helped the Babylonians overthrow the Assyrians and sacked their great cities of Nineveh and Nimrud. But in 550 BCE the Median king was deposed by Cyrus the Great, the most famous of all Iranian kings, and the Achaemenian dynasty began. In a fantastic and rapid

550 BC

killed in 530

series of conquests, Cyrus seized large swathes of Lycia and Anatolia in modern-day Turkey in the 540s BCE. In 539 BCE Cyrus captured the great city of Babylon, allowing him to take over much of that empire, including Palestine and Syria.

Cyrus, who was killed in 530 BCE while on a campaign, is still revered by many Iranians today. His monumental tomb at his capital of Pasargadae (near

Dari

the modern city of Shiraz) is still standing.

His successor Cambyses conquered Egypt, while Darius I then took the empire's frontiers to India, and it was under his rule that the empire reached its greatest

extent. He even built a canal between the Red Sea and
the Nile. But his most famous legacy is his building
at the city of Persepolis (known in Persian as Takht-e
Jamshid) near modern Shiraz. Many of the doorways,
stairways, and reliefs of Achaemenian soldiers and
other figures still stand and the site is one of Iran's
greatest tourist attractions.

It was also under Darius that the Graeco-Persian
wars started and with them the decline and fall of
the Persian empire. Seeking to make inroads into

Greece, the Persians found their match at the hands of the Greek states, which successfully halted the great expedition of Xerxes I, Darius's successor, in 479 BCE. Weakened both militarily and culturally, the Achaemenians could not withstand the invasion of Alexander the Great in 334 BCE.

The achievements of the Achaemenian empire still arouse strong passions. Some Iranian men still proudly bear the first names of Darioush (Darius) or Sirous or Koroush (Cyrus). The 2006 US film *300* about the Graeco-Persian wars that caricatured the ancient Persians as little more than bloodthirsty sadists sparked great anger in Iran—both from the government and among ordinary people.

Alexander the Great

Alexander overthrew the last Achaemenian king Darius III in 330 BCE. He is still reviled in Iran for his decision to destroy the buildings at the capital of Persepolis after his invasion. After his death in 323 BCE, Alexander was followed in ruling Iran by his general Seleucus who founded the Seleucid dynasty, under which Greek influence grew.

Parthians, Sasanians, and the Conversion to Islam

A nomadic Iranian tribe overthrew the Seleucids in the third century BCE and its kings became known as the Parthian dynasty. The Parthian kings, most notably Mithradates II, continued to grab territory, extending their hold as far as the Euphrates River. The Parthians were overthrown in 224 CE by the Sasanian dynasty, who were to rule Iran for the next four hundred years.

Until then, the ancient Iranian religion of Zoroastrianism had been widespread in Iran, but the

Zarathustra

Sasanians were the first Iranian dynasty to proclaim it the state religion. Most people in Iran converted to Islam after the Islamic conquest but, as we have seen, there is still a Zoroastrian minority to this day.

The Sasanian king Shapur I (240–72) was known for his religious tolerance and allowed Jewish, Christian, Manichaean, and Mandean minorities to worship freely. However, this was not the case under his successors. Under Shapur I, the Sasanian empire reached its greatest extent, with frontiers on the Euphrates River to the west and the Indus to the east.

Although less famous than the Achaemenians, the Sasanians were equally adept at conquering, and also left behind an impressive legacy of ancient sites such as their former palaces at Firouzabad in southern Iran and Ctesiphon in Mesopotamia. There are also stunning relief carvings such as those at Taq-e Bustan in Kermanshah province and works in silk, silver, bronze, and glass. Such was the demand, that Sasanian cut-glass objects were even traded as far as Japan.

But from 637 the Sasanian empire suddenly and rapidly collapsed after being defeated by the invading

Arab armies. They brought with them a new religion—Islam—which was to change the course of Iranian history forever.

The Spread of Islam and Shiism

Islam spread rapidly in Iran, perhaps indicating the weakness of the Sasanian dynasty on the eve of the Arab conquest. Islam had split into the Shiite and Sunni sects over a dispute as to who should succeed its founder, the Prophet Mohammad, who died in 632. Muslims who became known as Sunnis favored the caliphs, politically appointed nobles, to succeed Mohammad. Shiites, however, saw the succession to Mohammad as coming through his bloodline, starting with his cousin and son-in-law, Ali. When Ali's second son Hossein claimed the leadership after his death, he and his followers were massacred at the Iraqi city of Karbala on the order of the caliph Yazid in 680. Shiites still mourn this event fervently in streets and houses across the Middle East on the tenth day (Ashura) of the first Muslim month (Moharrem). (See Chapter 3.)

So-called "Twelver" Shiites, like those in Iran, recognize twelve imams stemming from Ali. The last of these—the twelfth imam, also known as the Mahdi—is believed to have disappeared into a state of "occultation" in 939. Shiites believe that he will return to the world to usher in a new era of harmony and justice.

Today, Shiites form the overwhelming majority in Iran and are also the majority in neighboring Iraq. There are further Shiite populations in

Bahrain, Kuwait, Lebanon, Egypt, Pakistan, and Saudi Arabia. But Iran, which was ruled by a succession of tribal dynasties after the conversion to Islam, did not become a Shiite state immediately. Shiites existed in Iran but Sunni worship was also widespread. It was only in 1501 that a new dynasty—the Safavids—ousted the Mongols who were then ruling Iran and began to zealously establish Shiism as the state religion. The emerging Shiite state in Safavid Iran rapidly became a counter and a rival to the neighboring Sunni Ottoman empire. The two sides fought numerous battles, further cementing the establishment of a Shiite identity in Iran.

As well as the monumental switch in religion, Safavid Iran also saw the building of road links, the expansion of industry, and an increase in diplomatic and trade links with the outside world. Its most famous ruler was Shah Abbas (1587–1629), during whose reign the great religious buildings and palaces in the imperial capital of Isfahan were completed. Finally sapped by the continuing wars against the Ottomans, Safavid Iran was conquered by the Afghans in 1722.

While Islam was rapidly absorbed, Iran was the only country in the first wave of the Arab conquests to retain its own language. Iranians are proud of their preservation of Persian, an Indo-European language whose structure has no relation to Semitic Arabic. Shiism, a minority Muslim sect, has also given Iran a religious identity distinct from its Arab neighbors.

The Qajars

In 1796 another tribal dynasty, the Qajars, came to power. Their rule, which was to last for the next 130 years, has earned a bad press from historians. Some Qajar monarchs have been seen as cruel, lazy womanizers, akin to the most excessive Ottoman rulers. The first Qajar ruler, Agha Mohammad Khan, is said to have plucked out the eyes of twenty

thousand men from the city of Kerman. During the Qajar era, the great powers Britain and Russia began a long struggle for control over the country they had realized was of crucial strategic importance. The noted Russian playwright Aleksandr Griboyedov was killed in Tehran by a mob in 1829 while on a diplomatic mission after seizing women from the imperial harem. The most prominent shah from the Qajar years, Naser ad Din, ruled ineffectually for forty-eight years. Concessions were also handed to Britain to exploit Iranian resources, starting a dangerous trend.

But if the shahs had other interests, reform did take place during this period at the hands of sometimes highly able bureaucrats. Naser ad Din's long-serving prime minister Amir Kabir founded the first schools of higher education and imposed economic reforms—even today his achievements are recognized in the name of Tehran's most prestigious technical university. Amir Kabir, who the shah had murdered while taking a bath, is one of the few administrators from the pre-Islamic Republic era whose name is still honored today.

Meanwhile, the state was forced to cancel a concession given to the British for Iranian tobacco in 1891 after mass demonstrations, the first time in Iran's history that protests had forced a government to back down. The tyrannical Qajar rule eventually led to pressure from dissatisfied merchants and clerics that resulted in the drawing up of Iran's first constitution and the convening of its first parliament in 1906. The movement known as the Constitutional Revolution ushered in the modern era.

Iran's Last Shahs, the Pahlavis

Dissatisfied with the weak rule of the Qajars, Britain in 1921 orchestrated a military coup, led by an officer of humble origins who had risen to command the Cossack brigade, Reza Khan.

Thus started one of the most controversial political careers in Iranian history. Forcing the creation of a new government, Reza Khan became war minister in 1921, then prime minister in 1923. In 1925 he declared himself shah and renamed himself Reza Pahlavi, after an ancient Persian language. Parliament voted for the abolition of the Qajar monarchy with only four against.

Drawing inspiration from Turkey's secular leader, Mustafa Kemal Ataturk, Reza Shah embarked on a campaign to modernize Iran economically, socially, and militarily. He reformed the army, introduced a new legal system, and worked to spread education. But his authoritarian rule left very little room for political debate. One of his most controversial moves was in 1936 to force women who wore the Islamic veil to go bareheaded. His police forces ripped off the head scarves and *chadors* (all-enveloping cloaks) of women who defied the order, something that the state media frequently remind Iranians of today.

Britain, meanwhile, was growing frustrated with Reza Shah's increasingly pro-German and even Nazi sympathies. Infuriated by his continued toleration of German agents in Tehran, Britain forced him to abdicate in favor of his son, Mohammad Reza Pahlavi, in 1941.

Mohammad Reza shared his father's authoritarian streak but few of his strengths. His rule saw massive spending to make Iran a great military power, the promotion of ties with the West, and a program of land reform. His so-called "White Revolution" sought to modernize Iran through land reforms, the spread of literacy, and improvements in women's rights. However, the reforms failed to create an affluent agricultural class and encouraged mass migration to the cities.

A monumental challenge to his rule came in 1953, when the Iranian prime minister, Mohammad Mossadeq, nationalized the oil industry to the fury of Iran's British and US patrons. Mohammad Reza fled the country, but Mossadeq was overthrown in a CIA- and British-backed coup that allowed him to return.

Mossadeq's defiance made him a hero for many Iranians. His secular tendencies meant his name was rarely mentioned in the early years of the Islamic Republic, but his defiance was frequently noted in the government's dispute with the West over its nuclear program. In the current standoff over Iran's nuclear program he is once again being recognized.

In 1971 the shah staged an outrageously lavish celebration at the Achaemenian capital of Persepolis to

mark what was touted as the 2,500th anniversary of the monarchy in Iran and where he sought to portray himself as the natural successor of Iran's ancient rulers. The event symbolized Mohammad Reza's excesses and his ignorance of the growing problems of the urban poor. Though he had labeled himself *shahanshahi* (king of kings), a mere eight years later he would be overthrown.

The Islamic Revolution and War with Iraq
The shah became increasingly unpopular as the growing numbers of urban poor saw no solution to

their problems. Dissent was crushed with increasing brutality by the secret police (SAVAK). The shah was overthrown in 1979 by a coalition of socialists, liberals, and Islamists led by the charismatic cleric Ayatollah Ruhollah Khomeini.

Khomeini had been a fierce critic of the shah since the 1960s and had been imprisoned, exiled to Iraq, and then France. He returned to Iran to declare his vision of an Islamic state. With the shah overthrown, Khomeini moved to sideline opponents of this vision and Iran became the Islamic Republic of Iran. Khomeini was the Supreme Leader of the Revolution, a position that, according to the new constitution drawn up after the Revolution, would always be held by a learned cleric. This idea of clerical leadership in state politics, or *velayat-e faqih* (guardianship of the jurist; pages 53–4), was one of the key ideas behind the formation of the Islamic Republic.

In complete contrast to the time of Reza Shah, veiling for women became compulsory and Islamic *sharia* law was imposed. But the new constitution also envisaged a presidency and a parliament that were to be directly elected by the people, albeit subject to certain controls. Thus the modern Iranian state is a combination of theocracy and democracy. While the West criticizes Iran for lacking freedom, its leaders still insist the country is a religious democracy (*mardomsalari-ye dini*).

The first years of the Revolution were tumultuous. The Islamic Republic's new leaders were targeted in bombings and assassination attempts by opponents of the regime who were still in hiding in Iran. All opposition was ruthlessly suppressed, and there were many executions. In late 1979 a group of Islamist students seized the US embassy in central Tehran and held its staff hostage for the next 444 days. The seizure reinforced the power of the Islamist radicals and also created a breach in relations with Washington that only now is seeing the most tentative signs of healing. The neurosis of the time, if not every historical detail, *to see!* is well brought out in the 2012 film *Argo*.

In 1980 the Iraqi dictator Saddam Hussein invaded Iran's southwestern Khuzestan province, which has an Arab population, in the hope of gaining possession of the oil-rich region. This resulted in a bloody eight-year war that is estimated to have cost a million lives on both sides. A successful Iranian tactic for repelling Iraqi advances was to send waves of often young volunteers on potentially suicidal missions into enemy fire. Iran finally accepted a UN resolution calling for a ceasefire in 1988, with both sides accepting a border agreement that had stood since 1975. War affected everyone in Iran due to food and fuel shortages and missile attacks that also hit Tehran. Few today do not know someone killed or wounded in the conflict. Saddam Hussein was notorious for his use of poison gas against Iranian troops, which has created a legacy of health problems for thousands of veterans. His hanging in 2006 was greeted with jubilation in Iran.

Reconstruction and Reform

When Khomeini died in 1989, his president, Ali Khamenei, was chosen to succeed him as Supreme

Leader. Iran embarked on a period of reconstruction (*sazandegi*) under its pragmatic new president, Akbar Hashemi Rafsanjani, who sought economic recovery after the destruction of the war. Some of the stricter social measures were softened but the economic recovery was marred by inflation and unemployment. Ties with the United States remained nonexistent and those with Europe thorny. Relations with Britain were cut for several years after Khomeini in 1989 issued a *fatwa* (edict) imposing a death sentence on the writer Salman Rushdie for his book *The Satanic Verses*.

After Rafsanjani had served the maximum two four-year terms as president, Iranians astonished the world in 1997 by choosing the reformist cleric Mohammad Khatami as his successor. For many of his young and often female supporters, Khatami offered the chance of a new start in a country with a booming youth population and he won a landslide victory. But while the smiling and articulate cleric impressed many in the West with his talk of a dialogue of civilizations, his attempts at broader political and social reform within Iran's Islamic system (*nezam-e*

Eslami) were stymied by powerful hardliners. In any case, Iranian reform (*eslah*) was primarily aimed at economic change and promoting foreign investment, accompanied by cautious social reforms. Despite winning a new mandate in 2001, Khatami left office in 2005, openly admitting he had failed to fulfill the hopes invested in him.

Ahmadinejad

Another election shock came in 2005 when Iranians elected conservative Tehran mayor Mahmoud Ahmadinejad (until then completely unknown outside Iran) as Khatami's successor. He crushed Rafsanjani in a runoff vote, winning the election on a mandate of promising to help Iran's poor finally feel the benefits of the wealth of OPEC's

number two oil producer. Early in his presidency, Ahmadinejad caused a storm by saying that Israel was doomed to disappear and downplaying the Holocaust. His style of diplomacy also raised eyebrows, as when he fired off personal letters to then US President George W. Bush and German Chancellor Angela Merkel. But most importantly, Iran headed into a standoff with the West over its nuclear program by reversing the suspension of sensitive activities agreed under Khatami.

The nuclear drive was a shah-era project that had been mothballed in the early years of the Revolution and then revived after Khamenei became Supreme

Leader. Whereas the West accused Iran of developing technology that could be used to make a nuclear weapon, Tehran insisted it was only seeking to provide electricity for its growing population. Ahmadinejad vowed, often in highly colorful language, never to back down on the issue and the UN Security Council imposed its first-ever sanctions against Tehran. The United States also refused to rule out military action.

Meanwhile, inflation increased and economists blamed Ahmadinejad for injecting excessive cash into the economy to fund local infrastructure projects. But the president, who proclaimed his government to be one of social justice (*edalat*), insisted he was doing all he could for the poor.

The 2009 Presidential Elections and Protests

The presidential elections held on June 12, 2009, proved to be a watershed moment in the history of the Islamic Republic, whose aftershocks are still being felt today. While still popular in some quarters, Ahmadinejad's populism and defiance of Iran's increasing international isolation were causing increasing discontent. A huge showing for a demonstration for Women's Day on March 8, 2009, underlined the tensions in society and potential for unrest.

The election campaign was marked by the stunning return to politics of Mir Hossein Mousavi, who held the now defunct post of prime minister from 1981–89 and was a close ally of Khomeini himself during the Iran–Iraq war. Never seen as a friend of his successor Khamenei, Mousavi disappeared from politics when the new Supreme Leader was appointed, concentrating on his passion for architecture, painting, and poetry. But after a twenty-year absence from politics, he threw his hat into the ring to stand as a broadly pro-reform candidate against Ahmadinejad.

Rumors buzzed through Tehran on election night that Mousavi had won a landslide victory and even that parliament speaker Ali Larijani—having seen the actual unpublished results—had telephoned him to congratulate. But the results when announced told a very different story. Ahmadinejad was reelected with almost 63 percent of the vote and Mousavi on 34 percent.

The supporters of Mousavi and his fellow reformist candidate Mehdi Karroubi were incandescent with rage, saying they had been robbed of victory by massive fraud. Hundreds of thousands took to the streets in the biggest anti-regime protests since the Revolution. The so-called Green Movement (*jonbesh-e sabz*, named after Mousavi's campaign color) shook the leadership. For the first time, opponents used social media networks to organize themselves The authorities responded with force, while Ahmadinejad supporters staged massive counter

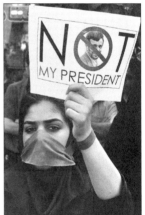

demonstrations. In an incident that was broadcast across the world after being captured on cell phone footage, a young woman named Neda Agha Soltan was shot dead in Tehran during a demonstration.

For a while it seemed Iran could be on the brink of a major convulsion, but the stern response of the security forces eventually slowed down the Green Movement. Demonstrations continued to be held, most notably after the death in December 2009 of the reformist Ayatollah Ali Montazeri, the one-time successor of Khomeini who had fallen out with his mentor. Demonstrations also resumed in 2011 in response to the "Arab Spring" revolutions in Arab states. It was at this point that the authorities arrested Mousavi and Karroubi and placed them after house arrest. Mousavi, his wife Zahra Rahnavard, and Karroubi remain under house arrest at the time of writing. They have never been put on trial or seen in public since. The publication in May 2014 of a rare photograph of Mousavi in hospital raised concerns for his health.

Ahmadinejad's Second Term and Nuclear Crisis
Ahmadinejad began his second term—the maximum consecutive mandate allowed under the constitution—with the country more polarized than ever, at odds with the international community over the nuclear program and the economy battered by sanctions. Most had seen Ahmadinejad as Khamenei's favored candidate in the elections and as the representative of Iranian conservative hardliners. But from 2009 an unexpected rift opened with Khamanei over one of Ahmadinejad's closest advisers, Esfandiar Rahim Mashaei, who conservatives accused of straying from Islam toward shah-style nationalism and even mysticism. Khamenei blocked Mashaei's appointment to first vice president and in 2011 vetoed Ahmadinejad's decision to sack the intelligence minister. Much to the amusement of many ordinary Iranians, Ahmadinejad then went into a ten-day "sulk," refusing to come to work or attend engagements. Ahmadinejad hoped Mashaei would run for

president in the next 2013 polls, but he was barred from running by the Guardians' Council.

Iran's relations with the world tumbled to new lows as Tehran was blamed for an alleged plot to assassinate the Saudi ambassador to Washington. On November 29, militant activists stormed the the British embassy and its residence compound in Tehran, prompting London to evacuate all its staff, shutter its operations in Iran and order the closure of the Iranian embassy in London. The embassy only reopened in August 2015 in what was seen as a major symbol of improving ties with Iran.

Nuclear Deal and a New Beginning?

Ahmadinejad's term limped to its end in 2013 with the president more a figure of fun than fear. With the nuclear-related sanctions now really biting into the wider economy, attention focused on the June 14, 2013, presidential elections. Rafsanjani, who had sympathised with the 2009 protests and seen his family hit by probes and trials, was barred from standing, in a sign of his marginalization from politics. Many expected a hardliner to sweep the polls and continue policies of increasingly risky but defiant isolation. But the 2009 protests had changed the mood in Iran. For the first time, the eight candidates held three US-style televized presidential debates that enthralled viewers in the country. In one of the biggest surprises in modern Iranian politics, the polls were won in a stunning first-round victory by the moderate cleric Hassan Rouhani, who crushed his nearest rival, the conservative Tehran mayor Mohammad Baqer Qalibaf, with almost 51 percent of the vote. Seen as a reformist committed to end Iran's isolation, Rouhani had been the chief negotiator in a 2003 nuclear deal with the EU and UN powers. Young people took to the streets of Tehran to celebrate his decisive—and undisputed—victory in boisterous scenes broadcast around the world. The contrast with 2009 could not have been greater. Was Iran on the verge of a new beginning?

Rouhani made clear his priority was to end Iran's international isolation and sanctions, which

had now extended to Tehran being cut off from the international SWIFT banking transaction system. Khamenei hardly encouraged the process but also did conspicuously little to block it. Occasional bilateral discussions were restored with the United States, and in

September 2013 US President Obama and Rouhani held telephone talks in the first such contacts since the Revolution. Showing off his reformist side, Rouhani opened a Twitter account, oversaw the appointment of a woman as foreign ministry spokesperson, and regularly espoused the need to respect the rights of citizens.

His greatest priority was to find a deal with the world powers on the nuclear controversy that would leave intact Iran's potential for an atomic energy program while allowing the dismantling of sanctions. After months of tortuous negotiations led by his English-speaking and charismatic foreign minister Mohammad Javad Zarif and US

...unterpart John ...rry, a deal ...s signed in ...enna in July ...15. Iran would ...it its nuclear ...tivities, and ...particular the ...nsitive practice ...uranium ...richment, which can also be used to make a nuclear bomb. Iran's compliance has been verified by the UN atomic agency, which will give the green light for the dismantling of the sanctions. This began on the so-called implementation day of January 16, 2016. Not all sanctions were lifted immediately but key restrictions on the oil and banking sectors were lifted and European companies are now licking their lips at the prospect of a vast market re-opening. Conservatives complain that Rouhani sold out Iran in Vienna, but many Iranians are relieved that their country now has a chance of being integrated into normal global life and ending its pariah status.

Tehran's aggressive foreign policy—which has seen it intervene in Yemen and Syria—continues to cause severe alarm in the West. Rights activists and journalists remain in prison. There should be no doubt that Khamanei, whose support of Rouhani has sometimes been lukewarm, is the number one. But for the first time since the false dawn of the Khatami era, there is cautious hope of a new beginning.

The Revolutionary Guards

The Revolutionary Guards of the Islamic Revolution (*Sepah-e Pasdaran-e Enghelab-e Eslami*) were formed shortly after the Revolution to merge several paramilitary forces and counter the power of the regular army. They are known to most in Iran simply as the *Pasdaran* (Guards). They are the most significant and most skilled military force in Iran and are regarded as its ideological army. Iran's best military hardware, including the Shahab-3 long-range missile that can reach Israel and southern Europe, is under their auspices. The Revolutionary Guards also control the *Basij* (Gathering), a volunteer militia claimed to number 12 million people. The head of the Guards is chosen by the supreme leader. With their own land, sea, and air forces, they played a key role in the eight years of the Iran–Iraq war and have remained prominent in all military areas ever since.

In recent years the Guards have expanded their activities in all areas of Iranian life. Ahmadinejad, himself a former member, promoted several former officers to cabinet posts. Dozens of MPs are former Guards, as is the mayor of Tehran, Qalibaf. As well as political influence, they have considerable economic clout, and their economic subsidiaries have seized major contracts in the energy, transport, and engineering sectors. Critics accuse them of profiting from the years of sanctions through illicit smuggling operations, and high-ranking members were among the most voluble opponents of the nuclear deal.

CITIES
Tehran

For most foreigners, Tehran is their first taste of Iran and it is not always the most palatable. A seething, polluted, traffic-filled metropolis, it is not an easy experience. The city has grown at a frenetic pace over recent years, putting a great strain on the infrastructure. The traffic, even by the standards of the Middle East, is abominable, and being stuck for hours on end in motionless jams is a common experience. The architecture is largely modern and uninspiring, with the exception of a few historic buildings in the south and north of the city. But Tehran has its redeeming features. It is the center of cultural life, and on a clear day the view to the north of the Alborz Mountains rearing up immediately above the city is spectacular. Tehranis also make up for the cold severity of the urban architecture with real warmth and hospitality. There are also a dozen or so very well-tended parks in the city center to escape from the chaos outside.

Isfahan

Isfahan is the ancient imperial capital of Iran built by Shah Abbas. It has the great Islamic and Persian architecture that Tehran painfully lacks and is a favored destination for foreign tourists. The massive

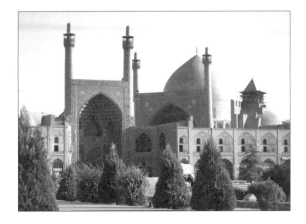

Naqsh-e Jahan Square, one of the largest in the world, is surrounded by a spectacular array of architecture. There are also impressive bridges and an atmospheric Armenian quarter. Nevertheless, liberal Tehranis are prone to look down on Isfahanis as conservative.

Qom

Qom is the clerical epicenter of Iran, home to the shrine of Massoumeh, the sister of the eighth Shiite imam, Imam Reza, and where the late Ayatollah Khomeini lived. Religion is all-pervasive here, and the city is dominated by clerics and seminary students and only very few women do not wear the all-enveloping black *chador*.

Mashhad

The holiest city of Iran, Mashhad, is home to the shrine of Imam Reza and is an important Shiite pilgrimage center. The city is also by far the largest urban conurbation in eastern Iran and its people are seen as canny operators, with many in positions of power throughout the country. Tehran's current mayor, Mohammad Baqer Qalibaf, hails from Mashhad.

Shiraz

The great city of southern Iran, Shiraz is a favorite with foreign visitors for its laid-back atmosphere and proximity to the great sites of Achaemenian Iran, such as the city of Persepolis and the tomb of Cyrus the Great at Pasargadae. It is also beloved of Iranians for its associations with the great medieval Persian poets Hafez and Saadi, who still exert a huge influence on Persian culture and are both buried in Shiraz.

Tabriz

The main city of northwestern Iranian, and freezing in winter, Tabriz has close trade and travel links to neighboring Turkey, and the Turkic Azeri language is more common here than Persian. While the city has few great monuments save an outstanding bazaar, it is situated in one of Iran's most beautiful regions.

Yazd

On the fringes of the desert in central Iran, Yazd is renowned for its still-inhabited and perfectly preserved mud-brick medieval city. Its maze of warrens and beautiful mosques are one of the great attractions of Iran. It is also the hometown of the former president Mohammad Khatami and is famous for its delicious sweets.

culture smart! **iran**

VALUES &
ATTITUDES

THE IRANIAN PSYCHE

National pride plays a huge role in what it means to be Iranian. Occupying a key position in the Middle East, Iranians are swift to remind foreigners that

they are not Arabs. The country is surrounded by Arab and Turkic states, giving Iranians a feeling of being unique in their own region. The atmosphere in the country is strikingly different from that of the Arab states, however near they may be. Iranians are very conscious of their own ancient history—there is a continuous connection between land and people going back thousands of years. Iranians will constantly refer back to the glories of the Persian empire as they still feel strongly this was achieved by their direct ancestors.

Iran is still a traditional society and religion plays a vital role in the identity of most of its people. The call of the mosque or a banner proclaiming love for an important religious figure is never far away. The fact that most Iranians adhere to the Shiite branch of Islam makes them feel distinct from the Arabs, most of whom belong to the majority Sunni denomination.

But Iranian society—unsurprisingly for a country of 80 million people and home to a number of different ethnic groups—is hugely complex. Indeed, making generalizations about this country is a risky business that has ensnared many in the media. Despite the international perception of Iran as a religiously conservative society, the reality is far more complex.

Iranians have a range of passionately held beliefs, interests, and pastimes. First-time visitors to Iran are almost always struck immediately by how lively urban society is; the streets are a gallery of exuberant activity. Music of all kinds, Western and traditional, blares out. People chatter away in a never-ending banter, the young try to impress with their style. Visitors should find people of both sexes who are ready to discuss (almost) any subject. Prepare to have any preconceptions about an unexciting, reactionary society well and truly dispelled.

RELIGION
Religion in Daily Life
The overwhelming majority of Iranians, normally estimated at more than 80 percent of the country's population, belong to the Shiite branch of Islam. As said above, for many people, whatever their political persuasion, being a Shiite Muslim is a fundamental part of being Iranian. Just because someone is Westernized, liberal, and secular does not mean that their religion is not an important part of their identity. Conversely, it would be wrong to assume that someone who is ostentatiously devout, possibly a turbaned cleric or a *chador*-clad woman, is inimically hostile to the West.

On religious holidays, shopkeepers rush out
into the streets to offer free drinks, fruit, and cake,
while the mosques are full all day long. If you visit a
major mosque on such a day, you will have a striking
indication of the importance of religious belief to
Iranians. It goes without saying that you should dress
conservatively and behave modestly, but generally
even on these intense occasions Iranians are happy
to welcome foreigners who show respect.

Atheists should bear in mind that Iran is not a
good place to express their beliefs. First, it is illegal
to do so in the Islamic Republic. More importantly,
Iranians in general, from all sections of society,
believe in God (*Allah* in Arabic, but Iranians
often use the Persian word *Khoda*) and would be
both astonished and perhaps even terrified by any
suggestion that God does not exist.

Shiites and Sunnis

That Shiism is so important to the national psyche
is perhaps explained by the fact that Shiites form a
minority within Islam, estimated to be between
10 and 15 percent of the world's Muslim population.

Shiites in Iran and elsewhere have customs, festivals, and rites that would be unrecognizable to adherents of Sunnism, the majority branch of world Islam.

As we have seen, the schism between the two sects dates from a disagreement over the successor to the founder of Islam, the Prophet Mohammad, after his death in the seventh century. Shiites recognize the Prophet's cousin and son-in-law, Ali, as his successor and thereafter the direct descendants of Ali. Sunnis, however, believed that political leadership and respect within the community were the most important prerequisites for a successor and recognized the rulers known as caliphs who went on to form the Umayyad dynasty in Damascus.

The first Sunnis were happy to separate religious and political authority, whereas Shiites believed that only the most exceptionally holy people could lead the Islamic community after the death of the Prophet. One and a half millennia later, the latter concept remains crucial to understanding how politics works in modern Iran.

For Shiites, the direct descendants of Ali, known as the imams, provide the necessary guidance for people to live in accordance with the precepts of God. The twelve imams are a feature of Shiite Islam that has no parallel in Sunnism. Iran sees scenes of fervent devotion during the holidays that mark the birthdays or death anniversaries of the main imams. (See Chapter 3.)

The Mahdi, Lord of the Age

Another special feature of Shiite Islam is the emphasis on the twelfth and final imam, known in Iran as the Mahdi or *imam-e zaman* (lord of the age). According to Shiites, the Mahdi is in a state of occultation after being hidden by God from the physical world in the tenth century. Shiites fervently believe in and wish for the Hidden Imam's return, which they believe will herald the end of time and the beginning of a new age of divine justice. In Iran, any mention of the name of the Mahdi is usually followed by the words "*Ajalallah ta'ala farajah*," "May God hasten his return."

The Cult of Martyrdom

Any visitor to Tehran cannot fail to notice the huge murals painted on the sides of office blocks and apartment buildings, frequently in prominent positions by major roads. Often brilliantly executed, they show fresh-faced young men with inscriptions in Persian. These men are the "martyrs" (*shahid*) of the eight-year war against Iraq, which came at a crucial stage early in the Islamic Revolution and remains key to the national psyche today.

Hundreds of thousands of men died in the war and their sacrifice is repeatedly hailed in speeches

and ceremonies by Iran's leaders today. In Western countries such a loss would be seen principally as tragic, but in Islamic Iran such "martyrdom" (*shahadat*) is seen as glorious and beautiful. A heroic death takes the soul to a blissful afterlife. This difference in cultural perceptions of conflict may demand a degree of sensitivity from the foreign visitor. In Iran, martyrs are to be worshiped, as shown by the cemetery for the fallen of the Iraq war (Behesht-e Zahra) just outside Tehran where a fountain eternally spouts red water symbolizing blood.

The war is known in Iran as the war of "Sacred Defense" (*Defa-ye Moghaddas*) and it is an incontestable historical fact that it was started when Saddam Hussein's forces invaded Iran's oil-rich west—Iranians will be very angry if you suggest otherwise. Many people you meet will have taken part in the war or lost loved ones.

The concept of the *shahid* goes back to the early days of Islam and the emergence of the bloody schism between Sunni and Shiite Islam. The most renowned martyr of all is Imam Hossein, who was killed at the battle of Karbala in Iraq and whose death is still marked each year by the impassioned Ashura ceremony.

Shrines

Also special to Shiite Islam are shrines, which are the burial places of the imams (the twelve successors of the Prophet Mohammad according to Shia Islam) and other important religious figures. Neighboring Iraq, which has a majority Shiite community, has a

number of important shrines, most notably in the cities of Najaf, Karbala, Baghdad, and Samarra. Iran also has sites of great significance, the most holy being the shrine of the Imam Reza in Mashhad. Another major site is the shrine of Massoumeh, Imam Reza's sister, in the central city of Qom. Khomeini has his own shrine just outside Tehran, a huge complex visible from the road to the new international airport.

NATIONAL PRIDE

All states in the Middle East show impassioned national pride, but in Iran it is something special. Pride in the country's ancient civilization, its natural beauty, and its cultural achievements is the one thing that unites all Iranians, whatever their political views and irrespective of whether they live inside the Islamic Republic or in the diaspora.

This national pride is shown in the questions that almost every Iranian will put to visitors about their experiences in the country and whether they were positive. They will be sure to ask whether you have seen its most famous ancient sites, like the ruined Achaemenian capital of Persepolis or the former imperial capital of Isfahan. They will also want to know how Iran compares with foreign countries. Days when the national soccer team is playing also show the intensity of this passion.

A reason perhaps for the intensity of national pride is the sense of historical continuity that modern-day Persians feel between themselves and their ancient past. Iranians see what their leaders always refer to as the "great nation of Iran" (*mellat-e bozorg-e Iran*) as going back thousands of years to the great Persian empire founded by Cyrus the Great in the sixth century BCE.

ABERROU

Nothing is more important in both the private and public life of an Iranian than pride. The notion is taken much more seriously than in the West and an episode that causes the loss of pride or "face," even if there is no material loss, is regarded as a catastrophe. In Iran, the idea is strongly conveyed by the word *aberrou*, which literally means "water of the face." Losing your *aberrou* in front of others is seen as an unmitigated disaster and Iranians of all classes will go to sometimes extraordinary lengths to ensure this does not happen. This can become very frustrating for outsiders, who may be given elaborate excuses rather than the truth just so that an Iranian can hold on to their *aberrou*. But in Iran, this is seen as perfectly normal and not lying in any way.

FATE

Fate (*sarnevesht*, or *ghesmat*) is another concept that may seem very abstract to outsiders but takes on a very real meaning in Iran. Even Iranians who do not profess to be religious can talk passionately about fate. The idea that the story of your life is somehow preordained (or "written ahead," which is what *sarnevesht* means) is hugely potent throughout Iran. If an Iranian survives injury or death, he is likely to ascribe his good fortune to fate rather than luck.

ATTITUDES TOWARD FOREIGNERS

Iranians generally adore foreigners. The country has had a long history of contacts with the West and it is only in recent years that it has found itself increasingly isolated on the international scene.

Foreigners have a degree of novelty value in Tehran that they do not have on the streets of Cairo or Dubai. People stop, look, want to ask questions. This may seem aggravating but the curiosity is relaxed and not in the least aggressive. Most foreign visitors leave Iran with a positive impression of the friendliness and hospitality of its inhabitants. They may even find themselves mobbed (in the nicest possible way) at famous tourist sites, with school groups excitedly asking questions and even begging for autographs.

Media coverage of Iran can sometimes give the impression of a society hostile to foreigners, but a quick stroll round any Iranian city—even somewhere very conservative such as clerical Qom—rapidly dispels these stereotypes amid smiles and handshakes. Of course, there are still sensitivities, and showing respect for the religious and national values outlined above will ensure that no offense is caused.

While almost all Iranians enthusiastically and genuinely welcome any foreigner (including Americans), many are also extremely bitter about the role played by Western governments in their country's history. They may even directly blame the West for ruining their business or failing to respect Iran's history.

For many, the country's potential has been held back by foreign states, either because of the invasions throughout its history or, in the previous century, the great powers' cynical rush to exploit its oil wealth. One date particularly etched in the mind of Iranians is the 1953 CIA- and British-inspired coup that toppled Prime Minister Mohammad Mossadeq after he nationalized Iran's oil industry to wrest it from foreign control. Iranians will passionately defend the country's right to nuclear energy but are also hopeful that the 2015 agreement with world powers over the controversial atomic drive will end years of isolation.

Most Iranians, whatever their views, are happy to draw a line between politicians and ordinary people, meaning foreign visitors can feel at ease. Many upper-middle-class Tehranis have relations living in the United States and Europe and can prove to be surprisingly familiar with these societies.

So Westerners are normally assured of a warm welcome. However, Iranians show far less respect toward the hundreds of thousands of Afghan refugees and migrants living in the country. Millions of Afghans have taken refuge in Iran over the past decade or so to escape the conflicts in their home country. They work on building sites and carry out menial jobs that no Iranian would be seen doing. They are often paid the most miserly of wages.

THE IDEAS OF THE ISLAMIC REVOLUTION

Iran's current system of government dates from the 1979 Islamic Revolution (see page 30). After the ousting of the shah, Khomeini moved quickly to suppress his erstwhile secular and liberal allies who did not share his worldview. Iran became an Islamic Republic (*Jomhouri Eslami*) whose laws and politics were based on Islam.

Nearly three decades after his death in 1989, Khomeini's personality and political vision still dominate Iran. His piercing eyes stare out from every banknote, his portrait hangs in every shop, his speeches are broadcast almost daily on state television. The country follows *sharia* law and strict Islamic values of clothing and behavior must be observed by the people in every area of public life.

Criticism of "Imam Khomeini," as he is referred to, is strictly prohibited. Massively charismatic, Khomeini was a complex figure who remains poorly understood in the West. Possessed of an extraordinary will to impose his vision, he was not without pragmatism when required.

Khomeini's political legacy is the system that runs the Islamic Republic, a highly personal vision known as the *velayat-e faqih* (literally, guardianship of the jurist). According to this system, the state is led both politically and religiously by a highly qualified cleric, who acts as guardian for the community in the absence of the twelfth imam. In line with this vision, Khomeini appointed himself Supreme Leader of the Islamic Revolution (*rahbar-e moazzem-e enghelab-e Eslami*). On Khomeini's death, he was succeeded in this position by the then president Ali Khamenei. Beneath the Supreme Leader, there are a number of bodies that work in line with the *velayat-e faqih*—the all-clerical Assembly of Experts (*Majles-e Khobregan*), which selects the Supreme Leader and is elected once every eight years, and the unelected Council of Guardians (*Shura-ye Negaban*), half of whose members are chosen by the Supreme Leader.

ISLAMIC VALUES, MODERN ATTITUDES
Iran has some of the strictest Islamic laws in the Middle East (with the exception of Saudi Arabia) but, ironically, perhaps the most colorful and diverse society in the region. Visitors often find that the picture of Iran they encounter as tourists or business travelers bears no resemblance to the "Axis of Evil" state portrayed in the Western press.

There *are* restrictions for sure. Women must cover their heads and all bodily contours. The consumption and sale of alcohol are strictly prohibited anywhere. Dancing is frowned upon and mixed-sex parties with Western music are illegal and sometimes the target of police raids. Sexual relations outside marriage are forbidden and theoretically punishable by jail sentences or even death. As in other Middle Eastern countries, kissing or other such contacts between partners in public is a complete no-no. Homosexuality is also strictly illegal (see more on page 99). Satellite television is banned as it is deemed to import decadence from abroad. The police regularly seize the dishes that are nonetheless a regular feature on some Tehran rooftops.

Iran executes more criminals annually than anywhere in the world other than China. Executions in Iran are almost always carried out by hanging. They sometimes take place in public, as well as in prison. Amputations and even stonings to death are allowed by law, if rarely carried out in practice.

But <u>Iran has loosened up considerably since</u> the late 1990s thanks to reforms, albeit cautious, and the effects of its huge youth population. The country presents a far more welcoming face to foreigners than in the decade after the Revolution, when the streets of Tehran were rocked by terrorism and the country was locked in a war of attrition with Saddam Hussein's Iraq.

The parks are now filled with young couples holding hands and quietly flirting. While many women still opt to wear the all-enveloping black *chador*, others, especially in Tehran, are pushing the limits of what is permissible, wearing figure-hugging coats and head scarves that show ample amounts of hair. <u>Mixed-sex parties, while illegal, do take place.</u> Political discussion can be lively, and it is not unusual for the government to be flayed in the reformist press for its policies.

WOMEN

Don't come to Iran expecting women to be shy, retiring types who never appear in the street. Anyone holding such beliefs will find them undermined pretty quickly. Indeed, within hours of arriving in Iran you are likely to have witnessed a scene like a female car driver giving a piece of her mind to a male fellow driver who she believes cut her off. Many people come to Iran expecting the position of women to be similar to Saudi Arabia, where it is even illegal for them to drive, but this simply is not the case. Women in Iran are well educated and opinionated. Many have successful careers, particularly in education, medicine and engineering.

However women have yet to make a major political breakthrough in politics in Iran. The current government has a sprinkling of women in prominent positions, notably foreign ministry spokeswoman Marzieh Afkham and one of the vice presidents, Massoumeh Ebtekar. Known as "Sister Mary," Ebtekar was the spokeswoman for radical students in the 1979–81 US embassy siege. But like many of her fellow hostage-takers, she went on to become a reformist politician and vocal critic of conservatives .

The most conspicuous aspect of women's lives in Iran is the Islamic dress code, under which a woman must cover her head and all bodily contours from the age of puberty onward. There are no exceptions and foreign women must obey the laws like any Iranian. This means female visitors must wear a head scarf and body coat anywhere in public, including hotel restaurants. As in other Islamic countries, the wearing of a *hijab* (head scarf) is seen by the authorities as a way of preserving a woman's dignity and preventing men having sexual thoughts about her in public. In winter, wearing *hijab* should not be too much of a hassle but some feel burdened by the extra clothing in the heat of Iran's summer. However, there is a huge diversity in what women wear on the streets (see more

in Chapter 4) and since the 1990s there has been a considerable relaxation over what is permissible.

Iranian men still expect women to do the cooking and clean the house, although richer families may hire help. A man usually will not help out in the kitchen, beyond doing the garden barbeque—although it's not impossible. The role of the woman in the home remains the traditional one of cook and housekeeper. However, such attitudes have not stopped women leading successful professional careers.

For a woman, blood money (*diyeh*)—the amount relatives can claim if a person is injured or killed in a crime or an accident—is set at half that for a man. A woman's testimony in court is worth half that of a man.

The awarding of the Nobel Peace Prize in 2003 to women's rights activist and lawyer Shirin Ebadi was a major symbol for Iranians of what women can achieve. Ebadi in the 1970s became Iran's first female judge, before women were banned from holding such posts after the Revolution. But she was able to resume work as a lawyer and took on sensitive human rights cases. The official response to her prize was at best lukewarm. In 2008, her Center for Defenders of Human Rights was raided by the authorities and shut down. With the official pressure making her work impossible, she has lived outside Iran since 2009.

Moral Crackdown

Stung by the perceived slipping standards, hardliners have launched sporadic moral crackdowns, with police targeting women whose dress is deemed inappropriate and other improper behavior. Women are warned that they are not obeying the dress code, while some men are apprehended for sporting "Western" haircuts or "decadent" clothing. Coffee shops—the traditional meeting places of boys and girls—have been shut down and shops selling inappropriate clothing raided. The police have insisted the crackdowns are popular with the public at large."Moral police" vans, marked in Persian as *Gasht-e Ershad* (Guidance Patrol), are a regular feature in Tehran's major squares. Male and female officers apprehend offenders and if necessary take them to a detention center to be given a written warning. Their parents then bring suitable clothing and they are released. Penalties for repeat offenders are stricter.

But the crackdown does not appear to have affected the dynamism of Iranian street society, which is here to stay. There is still a huge diversity of female dress on display in the streets and coffee shops are packed with couples on Thursday nights ahead of the weekends. There is no comparison with the stricter days of the early 1980s.

CUSTOMS & TRADITIONS

Iran has an astounding variety of public holidays, which in themselves reveal the country's complex and multifaceted history, with national days celebrating traditional pre-Islamic Persian festivals, Islamic holidays, and days marking the 1979 Revolution. In 2015–16 (the Iranian year 1394) Iran had twenty-two days of public holiday, making it one of the countries with the most public holidays in the world. Some of the religious holidays are celebrated by Muslims around the world while others are particular to Shiites and not marked by Sunni Muslims.

And on top of the holidays marked by days off, Iran commemorates several anniversaries with protests and other special commemorations.

THE CALENDAR

Iran's calendar is unique and very different from systems used elsewhere in the world. It is one of the most significant relics of the country's pre-Islamic past and still plays an important role in daily life. Don't expect January, February, March to mean much in Iran; you will have to learn the Iranian months and years as it is by these that all business is done.

The Iranian year, which is based on the sun, differs from both the Western solar calendar and the lunar calendar used in the rest of the Muslim world. In both the Persian solar and the Muslim lunar calendars, the years are counted from the flight of the Prophet Mohammad—to escape the persecution of Muslims in Mecca—to the sanctuary of Medina in 622, known in Arabic as the *hijra*. However, the start of the Iranian New Year is celebrated by a festival that is pre-Islamic in origin (Nowruz, see pages 64–6), marking the start of the vernal equinox, which comes around March 20. Thus the Iranian year between March 2016 and March 2017 is 1395, and then March 2107–March 2018 is 1396. All government and commercial business is done in line with this system, although of course Iranians are aware that the years are counted differently from other systems.

As the Iranian year is based on a solar calendar, important Muslim festivals, most notably the fasting month of Ramazan (Ramadan, see pages 69–70), change dates from year to year. The Muslim lunar calendar had been used extensively in Iran up to the twentieth century. However, Reza Shah made the ancient Persian solar calendar the country's sole calendar. Perhaps surprisingly, this usage has not been affected by the Islamic Revolution.

Iranians are proud of their calendar, which is

based on astronomical observations and has its own mechanisms for ensuring it does not fall out of synch. They are also proud of its claims to be the most accurate in the world and its origins in Persian history. The basic structure of the calendar is said to have been designed by a committee led by the great Iranian astronomer and poet Omar Khayyam in 1079. But it goes back further than that: the names of the twelve months in the solar Persian calendar have their origins in the ancient religion of Zoroastrianism. Their existence is perhaps the most obvious example of the continuing influence of Zoroastrianism—now a minority faith in Iran—on the daily lives of people in the Islamic Republic.

Six of the months are named after the metaphysical beings whom the Lord of Wisdom (Ahura Mazda) called upon to defeat hostile

Persian Month	Western Months	Named After
Farvardin	March–April	The descent of the guardian angels to earth
Ordibehesht	April–May	Lord of the Fire
Khordad	May–June	Protector of Waters, Health
Tir	June–July	Lord of the Scribe
Mordad	July–Aug.	Protector of Plant Life, Immortality
Shahrevar	Aug.–Sept.	Lord of the Sky, Stones
Mehr	Sept.–Oct.	Force of loyalty
Aban	Oct.–Nov.	Force of waters
Azar	Nov.–Dec.	Force of the fire
Dey	Dec.–Jan.	The Creator, in honor of Ahura Mazda
Bahman	Jan.–Feb.	Protector of Animals
Esfand	Feb.–March	Protector of Mother Earth

spirits. The names of four other months recall the mythological beliefs of the forces in nature that are beneficial to humans (for example, fire and water). One month recalls the guardian angels (*forouhar*) who descended to earth to protect mankind. Another month is named in honor of the Creator, Ahura Mazda, himself.

If you are spending any length of time in Iran, a knowledge of the calendar will be essential in coping with daily life. Sell-by dates on perishable goods, like yogurts and cheeses, all use the Persian calendar, while monthly remittances will be expected by the end of the Persian and not the Western month. In

Iran, the date is printed as year/month/day, usually using the Arabic numerals, although Latin numerals are now increasingly used instead.

Another good reason for learning the dates is the Iranians' habit of referring to important events in their history just by the date and not by what actually happened. For example, if you hear someone talking about the *bist-o do-e Bahman* (the 22nd of Bahman), they are talking about the day when the Islamic Revolution ousted Shah Mohammad Reza Pahlavi. In the same way, if someone mentions the *do-e Khordad* (the 2nd of Khordad), it is the day when Mohammad Khatami stunned the world by winning the 1997 presidential elections, stoking hopes of change and reform.

ANCIENT PERSIAN HOLIDAYS
Nowruz (starting March 20)

Nowruz, literally "New Day," is the Persian New Year and the most important holiday of the year for the majority of Iranians. Officially, the first four days of the New Year are a national holiday but in practice most people take off a fortnight and the country shuts down. The richest Iranians may head abroad but most people stream toward popular resorts inside the country and make a succession of family visits, which are obligatory over the New Year period. Thousands of Tehranis rush toward the north and the Caspian Sea to enjoy the bracing weather, leaving the capital unusually quiet, unpolluted, and for once free of traffic. Doing business is a bad idea at Nowruz as most people will be on holiday. It is also quite the worst time for tourists to visit the country as hotels will have been booked up months in advance by Iranians traveling or visiting relations. Transportation tickets will also be hard to come by in this period, with seats on long-distance trains particularly notorious for selling out the instant that they go on sale.

The Nowruz festivities are the only pre-Islamic festival still officially commemorated with a holiday in Iran. Some extremist clerics have called for it to be banned but such ideas have never been taken seriously by any government, which celebrates the holiday as enthusiastically as anyone else.

Nowruz marks the exact astronomical beginning of spring and is infused with symbols of renewal as well as Zoroastrian traditions dating back thousands of years. The most important tradition at Nowruz is the *haft seen* (seven "s"s), which correspond to the seven creations of the Zoroastrian faith and the immortals that protected them. Today, all these objects begin with the letter "s" but that was not always the case. They are *sib* (apple), *sekke* (coin), *senjed* (berry), *seer* (garlic), *sabze* (grasses), *serke* (vinegar), and *samanou* (a wheat meal). These objects are laid out on a table, where a plant is grown to celebrate renewal. A goldfish may also be bought to celebrate life. A Koran is added and also perhaps a book of poetry by the great medieval poet Hafez or the *Shahnameh* (Book of Kings), Iran's national epic by the poet Ferdowsi. There is also much cleaning of houses to mark the time of renewal. Traditionally, this is the time when all Iranians go out and buy a new set of clothes. This, as well as the general gift-buying, means the traffic in Tehran in the run-up to the festival is even more appalling than usual.

Chaharshanbe Souri (mid-March)

The New Year is preceded by a frenetic evening known as Chaharshanbe Souri (literally, Red Wednesday, not a public holiday). This takes place on the last Tuesday–Wednesday night before the New Year and could be described as an Iranian fireworks night. Its origins are not entirely clear, although the importance of fire during the celebrations has a parallel in Zoroastrianism. Fires are lit all over Iran, with the avowed aim of chasing away bad spirits. For most people, it is an excuse to throw firecrackers, light fireworks, and jump over bonfires. Predictably, people have been known to become over-excited and every year there are reports of injuries from burns or explosions. In the early days of the Islamic Revolution, Chaharshanbe Souri was frowned upon. But the authorities have recently allowed the celebrations to proceed in designated areas, albeit with stern warnings about public safety hazards.

Sizdah be Dar (April 1)

The New Year period officially ends thirteen days into the first month of Farvardin, with another uniquely Iranian festival celebrating nature, known as Sizdah be Dah (literally, the Thirteenth Outside) and also as the Ruz-e Tabia'at (Day of Nature). This is the day when all Iranians rush outside to go on spectacularly large picnics in nature, which can mean anything from the high mountains to a patch of grass by the roads. Town parks all over the country are filled with families sitting on rugs and drinking tea and eating Iranian specialties—it is one of the most atmospheric days of the whole Iranian year.

ISLAMIC HOLIDAYS

Ashura

The Shiite mourning festival of Ashura (named after the Arabic word for "ten") is perhaps the most important religious day marked in Iran. Coming on the tenth day of the Muslim month of Moharrem, Ashura marks the death of the third Shiite imam, Hossein, at the battle of Karbala in 680 in modern-day Iraq. Seen by his Shiite supporters as the true leader of the Muslims (being the grandson of the Prophet Mohammad), Hossein led a rebellion against the caliph Yazid I. Intercepted at Karbala, Hossein and almost all his supporters were slaughtered by Yazid's vastly more numerous army.

The martyrdom of Hossein still arouses genuine passion and even tears in Iran. These feelings reach their height during the mourning ceremonies of Ashura. Processions go through the streets led by drums and banners. Ashura is the time when the closeness between the Shiite faithful and their imams, even though one-and-a-half millennia have elapsed since the events took place, is particularly apparent.

The pain of the battle of Karbala and Hossein's mortal wounds are still felt as though they happened yesterday. Passion plays (*tazieh*) are staged to re-create the events of the battle, arousing great emotion among the spectators. Shopkeepers will put black mourning banners outside their shops, while taxi drivers have black pennants fluttering from the front of their cars. Many men wear black shirts, a sign of mourning in Iran. Some people flagellate themselves in an effort to empathize with the pain of Hossein and his followers. On occasion, passions during Ashura have run so high that people have been known to scar their heads and draw blood with knives. However, it is wrong to exaggerate this particular custom, which is frowned upon by the authorities nowadays and only practiced by a minority. For most people, Ashura is a time for reflection, prayer, and the family. It is not a celebration, however, and foreigners would be wrong to "congratulate" Iranian friends on the holiday. The day before Ashura is marked by the day of Tasua, meaning the ninth day of Moharrem.

Ramazan

Ramazan (Ramadan) is the Muslim holy fasting month. Like all other Muslims, Iranian Muslims are required to refrain from eating, drinking, and sexual activity from dawn until dusk. Seen by many outsiders as a period of sacrifice, Ramazan is also enjoyed by many Iranians for the time spent with the family and the huge feasts (*eftar*) that follow the breaking of the fast at sundown. Unlike in many

other Muslim countries, in Iran the consumption of food or liquid in public is strictly forbidden by law for everyone during daylight hours in Ramazan.

This makes Ramazan a difficult, though not impossible, time to travel in Iran. While restaurants will refuse to serve Muslims, some eateries in upscale hotels will discreetly serve non-Muslim foreign visitors. Shops are also open all day long throughout the month as normal, so it is easy to stock up on supplies to eat at home during the day. Travelers are exempt from the fasting rules and roadside restaurants remain open to all throughout the day. By no means do all Iranians strictly observe the fast all through the month, though a majority probably do so around the country. The key to enjoying the fast is said to be awakening before dawn for a large breakfast (*sahari*) and then avoiding too much strenuous activity before the evening *eftar* meal. As in other Muslim countries, business is slower in Ramazan and driving more erratic.

The fasting month ends with the Eid-e Fitr (festival of the Breaking of the Fast), which is usually marked in Iran with a two-day public holiday. There are major religious sermons on these days. But Eid-e Fitr is also a time for gift giving and eating. This is the time to congratulate Iranians on the festival, known in both Persian and Arabic as an *eid*, by saying "*Eid-e shoma mubarak!*" ("Congratulations on the festival!").

Birthday of the Mahdi
This is when Shiites remember their twelfth imam, the Mahdi, who they believe disappeared into temporary occultation in 939 and will return to save the world and usher in a new era of justice. Thousands of people make a pilgrimage to the Jamkaran Mosque, outside Qom, where he was once said to have appeared; from here, they send written messages to the Mahdi.

Arbaeen of Imam Hossein
From the Arabic word for forty, Arbaeen marks the fortieth day (as is traditional in Muslim mourning) after Ashura.

Eid-e Ghorban (Festival of Sacrifice)
This marks the near-sacrifice by Abraham of his
son, as recounted the Koran. Those who can afford
it sacrifice a sheep at home and distribute the meat
among the poor. There are also organizations that
take care of the whole process.

Eid-e Ghadir
This marks the appointment by the Prophet
Mohammad of Ali as his successor in Ghadir
al-Khumm in 632. However, Sunni Muslims do
not recognize that Mohammad made any such
appointment of a successor.

Martyrdom of the Imam Reza
The Imam Reza (Ali al-Ridha to Sunni Arabs) was the
eighth imam (successor) of Mohammad recognized
by Shiites. They believe that he was poisoned by the
then caliph in 818. His shrine in the eastern city of
Mashhad is one of the biggest mosques in the world.

The other Islamic holidays are: the martyrdom of
Ali, the birthday of Ali, the birthday of Mohammad,
the death of the Prophet's daughter Fatimah, and the
ascension (*Shab-e Meraj* in Persian) of Mohammad to
speak to God in 621.

ISLAMIC REVOLUTIONARY HOLIDAYS
The third kind of national holiday in Iran relates to
the events of the 1979 Islamic Revolution.

Victory of the Islamic Revolution (February 11)
This is the major revolutionary holiday, held to
celebrate the day in 1979 when the shah's army refused

to intervene to put down the popular uprising against the imperial regime. Although the shah had left Iran three weeks earlier, this is now considered the day that he was toppled. The holiday is marked by gigantic rallies of hundreds of thousands across the country and much chanting of the mantras of "Death to Israel!" ("*Marg bar Israel*!") and "Death to America!" ("*Marg bar Amrika*!"). Superficially it all sounds very hostile, although nowadays the marches have more of the atmosphere of a fiesta with sports exhibitions, face painting, and balloon displays encouraging families to take part. The ten days leading up to February 11 are known as the *Dah-e Fajr* (Ten Days of Dawn). This period also sees Iran's main film festival, known as the Fajr Film Festival.

Oil Nationalization Day (March 19)
One of two public holidays in Iran marking an event in its shah-era imperial history. Oil Nationalization Day commemorates the move proposed by prime minister Mohammad Mossadeq and agreed by parliament to nationalize the Iranian oil industry in March 1951, and end the monopoly enjoyed by the British-owned Anglo-Iranian Oil Company (AIOC). The US and Britain reacted furiously, staging a coup in 1953 that ousted Mossadeq and shored up the waning powers of the shah. Mossadeq's decision to give Iran control over its own energy resources took on a new significance in the modern Islamic Republic amid the standoff over the Iranian nuclear program, and is seen as a victory for a self-sufficient Iran over colonialism. Many historians outside Iran now see the ousting of Mossadeq as

a fatal mistake by the West, paving the way for
the Islamic Revolution by removing a moderate
nationalist secular leader who could have ruled
the country effectively.

Day of the Islamic Republic (March 31)
This national holiday marks the overwhelming
support given by Iranians to the idea of declaring
Iran an Islamic Republic in a referendum on
March 31, 1979.

Death of Ayatollah Khomeini (June 3)
This major mourning holiday marks the death of
Khomeini in 1989. Black banners fly above the
streets, the papers publish special supplements
devoted to the man known simply in Iran as "the
Imam," and state television relays his speeches.
Major ceremonies amid a huge crush of people
are held at his shrine south of Tehran, including a
speech by the Supreme Leader.

Khordad Uprising (June 5)
In 1963, Ruhollah Khomeini was gaining
prominence as an opposition force in Iran with
his anti-shah teachings from his base in Qom. In
June 1963, his arrest by the SAVAK secret police
sparked protests in Tehran that spread nationwide.
They were suppressed with the use of massive
police force leading to the loss of hundreds of
lives. The event is today remembered by the
Iranian holiday 15 Khordad—the Iranian date
when it took place—which is seen as the first
major challenge to Shah Mohammad Reza Pahlavi
on the streets. This time he was able to regroup,
but not in 1979.

OTHER COMMEMORATIONS
Week of Sacred Defense (end September)
The week of "Sacred Defense" (*Defa-ye Moghaddas*) recalls the start of the Iran–Iraq war in 1980. The week of ceremonies kicks off with a huge military parade in Tehran where most of the country's weapons are on display. The week is a time of rousing speeches from politicians and the military recalling Iranians' readiness to defend their land, something that has gained added pertinence amid the tense nuclear standoff with the West. But it is also a time for remembering wounded veterans or those who have lost loved ones.

"Nest of Spies" Occupation (November 4)
This commemorates the day in 1979 when radical students stormed the US embassy in Tehran, dubbed the "Nest of Spies," and held more than fifty US diplomats and marines hostage for the next 444 days. In the Islamic Republic, the seizure of the embassy is still feted as a heroic revolutionary act

and demonstrations are held across the country. The most important is held outside the former site of the US embassy, in downtown Tehran, where the siege took place. Thousands of students gather to chant "Death to America!" and burn effigies of Uncle Sam. Despite the hard rhetoric, any visiting foreigners are likely to be treated with benign curiosity and laughter rather than hostility.

The hostage siege was of great significance: it further radicalized the Revolution and sidelined relative moderates like pragmatic prime minister Mehdi Bazargan, who was forced to resign. The seizure of the embassy caused a rupture in Tehran–Washington relations that has yet to be repaired. But many of the leading student radicals in the hostage siege went on to become reformist politicians pushing for change in the Islamic Republic.

chapter four

MAKING FRIENDS

FRIENDSHIP IN IRAN

Making friends as a foreigner seems extremely easy in Iran. Everywhere you go, people will want to engage you in conversation, ask you about your country, and want to know what you think of Iran. You will be showered with invitations to tea and meals and even given gifts (postcards and other souvenirs) by complete strangers. This is partly because the idea of friendship (*dusti*) is valued highly by Iranians. War and economic problems have meant that life has not been easy for many people over the last years and they have learned to count on each other. Iranians proudly say how strangers will immediately stop to help if they see a car broken down or someone in trouble.

Perhaps the most important friends are within the

extended family—families in Iran are usually extremely close units (see Chapter 5), who come even closer together at times of celebration, such as births, and mourning. It is quite a widely held view in Iran that families there are much closer and more loyal than families in the West—they could be right. Both men and women are also likely to form close bonds with classmates at school and university that last for life. These are loyalties that can also leave their mark in professional life.

While like anywhere else it pays to be streetwise, don't be distrustful of seemingly spontaneous kindness. In Iran, it is often for real, with no ulterior motive. Shopkeepers might offer sweets, an Iranian tourist might insist on buying you a postcard as a souvenir, or a fellow passenger may with a smile quietly pay your shared taxi fare.

Of course, it is one thing to make acquaintances and another to make friends. In Iran, making genuine friends as a visiting foreigner, like any other country in the world, is not always straightforward. Western visitors are likely (although not always) to be considerably richer than Iranians they meet and the question of money can always cause underlying strains. Despite the similarities to life in Europe and the United States, some aspects of Iranian culture (*farhang*) are very different and breaking this barrier takes time, understanding, and effort.

As previously mentioned, Western countries have not always played the most noble role in Iran's history and this can lead to suspicion. Above all, many Iranians in the workplace are understandably bitter that foreigners on assignments earn several times as much as they do despite perhaps having similar qualifications. Foreigners working for embassies, media groups, or oil firms come and go but it is the Iranians who stay and form the backbone of the operation. A foreigner can also leave the country very quickly if necessary, an option that is not open to most Iranians. But if you succeed in overcoming these issues, a friendship made in Iran is something to be treasured and it will likely last for life.

INTERACTING WITH IRANIANS

Given the sharp words that are frequently flung between the Iranian government and the West, a visitor might expect to be regarded with suspicion and

even hostility in public. There *is* lots of anti-Western rhetoric in public in Iran—just listen to the shouts of "*Marg bar Amrika!*" (Death to America!) chanted by worshipers after Friday prayers, for example. This is sometimes extended to include "*Marg bar Inglistan!*" ("Death to England"— curiously, the slogan "Death to Britain!" does not exist) or whichever country is currently out of favor with the Islamic Republic. State media and the country's leaders repeatedly slam the "bullying" of Western powers and the "lies" propagated by the Western media.

But such rhetoric should not trouble foreign visitors, who should remember that it's a matter of politics, directed at governments and not at individuals. Even the people chanting these slogans would probably be delighted to engage in a political debate with a Western visitor, providing the language barrier can be overcome. Look at people's faces during an anti-Western demonstration such as the one marking the victory of the Islamic Revolution and you will discover smiles rather than hostility. It is possible the 2015 nuclear deal will also eventually tone down the rhetoric.

For the most part, Iranians have a great curiosity toward foreign visitors. They are well-educated and well-informed and it's not unusual to be accosted by someone who wants to discuss the finer points of Western literary traditions with you. They are also not afraid of talking politics, be it about Western countries or their own.

It is refreshing to find that in modern Iran people have little fear of talking to foreigners. In theory, Iranians could be arrested for having "contacts with foreigners" but this usually refers to accusations of passing secrets to foreign embassies. In the streets at least, ordinary people are astonishingly ready to say what they think about the economy, the government, or world powers. It is interesting to see how many people, often strangers, discuss the important political questions of the day on public transportation.

MAKING CONVERSATION IN PERSIAN
Basic Phrases

Making some basic conservation in Persian will endear you to almost everyone in Iran and make you an instant celebrity. The traditional way of saying hello is "*salaam*," although some people use the full Arabic "*salaam aleikom*." Depending on the time of day, you can wish someone "*sobh bekheir*" (good morning) or "*shab bekheir*" (good evening). "Yes" in Persian is "*bale*" (with the stress on the first syllable, as in "ballet"), though in colloquial speech "*areh*" is often used. "No" is "*nakheir*," though in speech this is almost always shortened to "*na*."

As in the Arab world, no one would even think of starting a conversation without inquiring after the other person's health. It's not normally necessary to reply; the most important thing is to make the same inquiry in return. Having got this out of the way, you can then attack the matter at hand. The normal openings for a conversation are "*Hal-e shoma*?" (How are you?) or just "*Shoma khoub-i*?" (You are fine?). You might reply "*Man khoubam*" (I'm fine) or "*Bad nistam*" (I'm not bad). It will not be long before the curious ask "*Shoma ahl-e kodoum keshvar hastid*?" (Which country are you from?) to which you might reply "*Man az Amrika hastam*" (I'm from the United States). People will likely want to know what you think of Iran, and will be delighted by a positive answer. "*Iran ra kheli dust daram*" (I love Iran) or "*Iran kheli khub-e*" (Iran's great!) is likely to bring a smile to Iranians' faces. Some may complain that the government (*dowlat*) in Britain or the United States is *bad*, or about the domestic *eghtesad* (economy).

This being Iran, personal questions will follow with surprising rapidity, especially the inevitable "*Shoma ezdevaj kardid*?" (Are you married?). It is also considered normal to ask "*Hoghug-e shoma chand-e*?" (How much are you paid?). People will also be very curious to know "*Mazhab-e shoma chi-ye*?" (What is your religion?) to which the stock answer for most Westerners will be "*Man masihi-am*" (I'm Christian). Having exhausted these possibilities, it might be time to switch to another language. The phrase "*Shoma Englisi balad-id*?" (Do you speak English?) will be useful.

The biggest obstacle in making friends is the language. Some Iranians, especially in Tehran, speak perfect English or possibly French or German. People who want to practice will inevitably latch on to you. In other situations, however, you may find people's grasp of English is rudimentary or nonexistent.

Don't Be Tired!

The most idiosyncratic of colloquial Persian phrases is "*Khasteh naboshi!*", which translates as "Don't be tired!" Its use is ubiquitous. The phrase is used essentially as a greeting to anyone doing any kind of work—this could be in an office, in a restaurant, playing sports, or climbing a mountain. Of course the person addressed may be extremely tired if they have been working, but in the polite world of Iranian society this seems not to matter.

Iranians are often curious to find out what the equivalent of "*Khasteh naboshi!*" is in English but the simple truth is that there is no good translation for this most Persian of concepts. Some Iranians dislike the expression, seeing it as imposed after the 1979 Revolution.

A very good way to integrate socially in big cities like Tehran is to join the thousands of people from all social classes who take picnics high into the hills on a Friday. Any foreigner is likely to have numerous invitations to join a picnic or play a spot of volleyball and it's a great way to meet like-minded people—so long as you have the stamina for the steep mountain trails. Expect to be told "*Khasteh naboshi!*" very many times!

Conversation Topics

Many Iranians, especially men, are fanatical soccer fans, and may be better informed about the European leagues than foreign visitors. This is because most top European games are broadcast live and free to view on Iranian state television. Be prepared, if you can, to wax lyrical about the European game, say what your favorite team is, and talk up the prospects of the Iranian national side.

As mentioned above, Iranians have far fewer scruples about asking personal questions than in the West. It is relatively normal to ask how much a foreigner's salary is or how high their rent is. One of the first questions you will have to field is whether you are married. If the answer is "no" be prepared for a follow-up "*chera*?" (why?)—Iranians have a horror of staying unmarried above a certain age and cannot understand why a foreigner would want to remain single voluntarily.

Politics also looms large in conversation, be it the situation in Iran or outside. All Iranians are also happy to talk for ages about the country's attractions, be it the excellent climate, its ancient sites, or the beauty of cities outside Tehran. The congested capital's inhabitants have a great enthusiasm for the lush and rainy north (*shomal*) of the country and are not shy in recommending that foreigners should visit there.

PERSIAN NAMES

The variety and descriptiveness of many Iranian names make those used in the West seem dull by comparison. Of course, many people in Iran have Islamic or Arabic names. The most popular names for men might be Mohammad after the Prophet himself, or Ali and

Hossein after his descendants. Reza, after the eighth Shiite imam, is also very popular. Many women are called Fatemeh (Fatima) after the Prophet's daughter or Massoumeh after Imam Reza's sister.

However, there is a multitude of names of Persian origin that are still frequently used in Iran. For men, many of these come from heroes of the national epic the *Shahnameh* by Ferdowsi, such as Arash, Babak, or Siavash. Omid, meaning hope, is a boy's name. Sirous and Koroush are two versions of the name of Cyrus the Great. Shahab is a meteor. Some widely used names also recall biblical prophets who feature in the Koran such as Ebrahim (Abraham), Yahya (John), and Issa (Jesus).

For women, the choice of names seems even wider. If for men the main source of Persian names is the *Shahnameh*, then for women it is flowers (for example, Lili, Narguess, Nasrin, or Shaghayegh). But women may also be named after planets, ideas, or precious stones. Other popular names include Bita (unique), Forough (brightness), Zohreh (Venus), Souzan (flame), and Elham (inspiration). As a boy can be called Omid (hope), a girl may be called Arezou (wish).

On marrying, Iranian women do not usually take their husband's surname and keep their maiden names for the rest of their lives, although of course both sons and daughters will take their father's surname.

SOCIAL CUSTOMS

Understanding the elaborate social rituals that underpin most human interactions in Iran will go a long way toward making you feel at home in society. It is also important to find a balance between respecting the Islamic rules that are the laws of the country and feeling relaxed in a modern society.

Ta'rof – **When No Means Yes**

One of the most confusing and potentially awkward social customs for the foreign visitor is *ta'rof*—the polite rejection of something one actually wants to receive. Initially this may seem unnecessary and insincere but it is an integral part of all interactions in Iran and underlines the importance of courtesy in the culture.

You are in a taxi, for example, and at the end of the ride you offer to pay—the driver may look at you in mock horror and say "*Mehmoun-e man bash*" (Be my guest) or "*Befarmian!*" (Please!). Of course the driver has a living to make and does want your money; he is just being polite. You should insist on payment three times and on the third the driver will invariably take your money with a grateful smile.

The same principle operates in shops, restaurants, hair salons, or anywhere where money changes hands. It is important to master *ta'rof* if you are staying in Iran for any length of time. Tales abound in Tehran of foreign residents who gratefully ran off without paying when their barber or taxi driver made *ta'rof* by pretending to refuse payment. The foreigner probably left with the most wonderful picture of Iranian generosity, but the poor barber or taxi driver was left empty-handed. Iranians are hospitable but don't expect to be offered basic services free!

Sometimes *ta'rof* can reach bizarre extremes. For example, a taxi driver in Tehran, perhaps of the more unscrupulous breed, may first refuse payment and then once you pay him tell you bluntly you have not paid enough. Then when you offer the extra sum, he will again make *ta'rof* before accepting the additional notes. It's all part of the daily ritual of Iranian life.

Curiosity
Iranians are also hugely curious (*fouzoul*). Without much preamble, they are happy to ask intimate question about salaries, love life, and rents. They love to gossip, often about other people, and the parks at weekends are filled with families and friends taking a stroll while animatedly talking. In days gone by, there was a quaint custom at New Year known as *falgoush* (fortune hearing), where people would secretly eavesdrop on strangers' conversations and use them to tell their own fortunes. The custom is said to have been particularly popular with young women wondering if the New Year would see them meet a husband. Unsurprisingly, *falgoush* is now deemed socially unacceptable and has become almost extinct.

To Shake Hands or Not?
Iranian men are inveterate handshakers and you should shake hands even with close acquaintances whom you see every day. Handshakes between men and women are a more complicated issue. In theory, it is forbidden (*haram*) for people to have any bodily contact with members of the opposite sex in the Islamic Republic. Former presidents Ahmadinejad and Khatami were both attacked by the hard-line press when they were photographed making rare handshakes with women. With foreigners, however, the rules seem a little more permissive and no one will arrest you in Iran for shaking hands with a woman.

The golden rule for a Western man is let the woman take the initiative; in other words, don't create an embarrassing situation by offering your hand to a woman who does not want to shake it. However, if a more Westernized woman does offer you her hand, it would be considered petty and insulting to refuse it. Iranian women are well educated and nowadays perhaps more likely to speak a foreign language than men, given they form the majority at colleges and universities. They are articulate and opinionated about their country and male visitors should not be shy about engaging them in conversation, while respecting the culture at the same time.

A good gesture to use in any situation is to place your right hand on your heart. This can be used to mean many things: that you are touched by a gesture, that you are pleased to meet someone, or that you have enjoyed your meal but have eaten enough. It is also a very useful gesture to use when greeting a woman if it is deemed inappropriate to shake hands.

Male Dress

One thing that is not necessary in Iran is to dress up too much. Ties are generally frowned upon—although not illegal—as they are seen as a symbol of Western imperialism. Most officials generally content themselves with an open-necked shirt and jacket and will probably appreciate it if you dress in a similar way. You may see some people who work for private businesses wearing ties, but it is still not common. Ties were popular for the upper and middle classes before the Islamic Revolution and today they are still used when men want to dress up particularly well for a wedding party or major private celebration.

Dress to Impress: What Women Wear in Iran

Some foreign women do the very minimum to obey the dress laws in Iran, maybe just wearing a bandana as a head scarf and a long shirt. But whatever one's personal views, such behavior will not impress the more conservative elements and may encourage unwelcome stares from men. Foreign female visitors are better off dressing like a modern Iranian woman and this can be brought off in a way that is perfectly stylish and will make you feel much more at ease in Iranian society.

The more conservative women in Iran wear the *chador*, which literally means tent and is a single wraparound garment that envelops the body from head to toe, leaving only the face and hands visible. It's worth noting that hardly any women cover their face completely. The *chador* is not easy to wear and women frequently have to readjust the folds in the street to ensure they are properly covered. The only situation where a foreign woman might wear this garment would be in a mosque or at some other holy site. Otherwise you'd be crazy to wear it as it's not compulsory and Iranian women would simply laugh at you!

Foreigners are better off with a *manto*, a long, thin coat that goes down to the knees and does the job of obeying the dress laws while being comfortable and possibly stylish. You don't have to wear black—nowadays all manner of colors and styles are available and perfectly acceptable. The garment should not be body-hugging tight but foreigners are likely to be allowed more leeway in these matters than native Iranians. You can easily buy a *manto* in any shopping center for little more than US $10.

This of course should be topped off by the *hijab* (head scarf). Again, you will see a huge range of colors and styles on the streets. It can be tied under your chin but many Iranian women wrap shawls around their heads, which may seem more stylish. There is also the *maghanae*, a kind of ready-made *hijab* that you just throw over your head and covers well below the shoulders. It's normally black, dark blue, or green and worn by students and schoolchildren. A foreigner normally would not wear it but it does have the advantage of not needing to be tied or adjusted.

VISITING AN IRANIAN HOME

An invitation to an Iranian home is a great honor and is likely to be a highlight of any trip. Iranians are proud of their hospitality and will go to great lengths to look after a *mehmoun* (guest), especially a foreign one. Here you will see people relaxed and outgoing, away from the rules that prevail on the street.

It is considered polite to bring a gift: normally a box of *shirini* (sweet cakes or cookies) although if you've brought any choice tea from back home this will be appreciated even more. It goes without saying that before entering the house you should remove your shoes. You might be offered slippers but it's perfectly acceptable to walk around in socks and it's also comfortable given that most Iranian homes are covered in wonderful carpets.

Most meals will start with the first of many offers of tea. In a legacy of the cultural and political influence Russia had on Iran in the nineteenth century, tea is brewed in a *samovar*, the traditional Russian tea urn. Water is boiled in the lower chamber and this is then added to the strong tea brewing on top. You will then be presented with a glass bowl to choose from a glistening array of fresh sweet cucumbers and tomatoes and then another bowl with fruit. (In Iran, it's perfectly normal to eat fruit before your meal.) These are normally eaten with a knife and fork from a small plate. You'll also be offered a vast array of nuts and dried fruit, so it's quite possible to fill up before the meal has even begun.

The meal proper in some households, especially more traditional ones, may be served simply on a sheet on the floor (*sofreh*), with the diners seated around with their legs crossed. Eating from this position while not putting your face in the food or dropping any on the floor proves uncomfortable for many foreigners. However, Iranian hosts are extremely sensitive to any discomfort on the part of their guests and will set up a small table if you are unable to master eating on the floor. This can be somewhat embarrassing if you are alone at a table. But in any case, better-off households, especially in Tehran, would not think of eating on the floor and take all meals seated as a group at a table.

The food will keep on coming, so make sure you have arrived hungry. There is likely to be a selection of kebabs and stews as well as a huge plate of Basmati rice. Iranians normally eat the main course with a spoon and fork, and no knife. For dessert, expect delicious Iranian cakes followed by fruit and sweets and yet more offers of tea. You will need some time to digest. Choose the right moment to leave—not too soon but also not too late as no Iranian host would dream of even dropping a hint to a guest that it's time to go. Generally, most dinner parties will start to break up around midnight.

chapter five

PRIVATE & FAMILY LIFE

IRANIAN HOUSES AND APARTMENTS

Half a century ago, better-off Iranian families could have expected to live in palatial bungalows with large gardens. But this changed with the huge demographic changes in recent years. All but the super-rich in Iranian cities live nowadays in apartment blocks.

For low-income earners, home means a tiny flat, but the rich may have a luxurious apartment with a shared swimming pool, underground parking garage, gym, and sweeping views. The last years in Tehran especially have seen an unprecedented construction boom. The old Qajar-era bungalows, which often had large gardens, have been mercilessly ripped down and replaced by huge towers (*borj*) that can accommodate hundreds of people. There is barely any spare ground left in leafy northern Tehran that is not being turned into a modern development.

The capital has now become an urban megalopolis with the migration from the provincial towns (*shahrestan*), creating a population that has now reached at least 8 million in the city and as many in the wider suburbs whose individual identities have now been swallowed up. Satellite towns like Karaj to the west have lost their distinct identities and become dormitories for workers from the capital, with populations already in the millions. As a result, the face of Tehran has changed beyond all recognition and older residents will often reminisce nostalgically about how peaceful and bucolic the city was in former times.

For all Iranians, the price of property (*maskan*) has become a major problem in recent years as the move from country to city fuels a huge demand for urban dwellings. Prices for the best apartments in Tehran are already in the millions of dollars and easily comparable with those in a Western city. Even buying a modest first apartment may be out of reach for a young middle-income buyer. It has become fashionable for first-time buyers in Tehran to purchase property way out in the suburbs where it is cheaper and rent it out as an investment while continuing to live with their parents.

THE IRANIANS AT HOME
Amid all the urban difficulties created by overpopulation, Iranians keep their homes very separate from the outside. Being welcomed inside

someone's house from the stressful chaos on the streets is like entering a different world. In few countries is there such a strong division between the public and private worlds, a phenomenon accentuated by the society's strict Islamic rules.

The Living Room

In almost all households, Persian carpets will be the key element of furniture. They are used for sitting on,

 relaxing on, and eating off (with the addition of a protective plastic sheet). Little of the actual floor is usually visible, such is the enthusiasm for the carpet. Their use gives an Iranian home a much more spacious look than a Western apartment and it is usually free of clutter. It also means that in almost all cases guests should remove their shoes before entering the house. This protects the carpets and is in line with the Iranian abhorrence of dirt from the street entering the home, as in any Islamic society.

Surrounding the carpet will be chairs, which is where visitors will be encouraged to sit. A small low table will usually be covered with huge bowls of nuts and fruit, which is the absolute minimum that is offered to any guest, along with tea. They are normally eaten with small plates and knives. There will be at least one sofa in almost all houses. And of course a television, which will invariably be kept on all day. The kitchen is the undisputed realm of the lady of the house.

The Bathroom

Toilets in the more luxurious apartments will be Western-style but those in less fancy places could be of the squat kind. In any case, there is likely to be a choice between toilet paper and the more traditional water hose (attached to a tap next to the toilet) for cleaning. Iranians do not worry about spraying water all over the bathroom during showers and ablutions and guests will always be advised to put on a pair of plastic sandals before entering.

Public and Private

Iran imposes strict rules on behavior in public and there is sometimes a noticeable difference between how relaxed people are in public and in private. Although this was not the case in the first years of the Islamic Revolution, the authorities nowadays usually do not interfere with what people do in private behind closed doors. Raids on mixed-sex parties (formally illegal) do still take place, but with less frequency than before, and usually because of complaints about noise from neighbors. This means that the private home is the place to relax and talk freely. In Iran, the best night out is considered to be attending a dinner or a party (*mehmouni*) at the home of a friend. Iranians strongly protect the privacy of their home and most apartment blocks will have closed circuit television to identify any unwelcome intruders. Apartment blocks and houses are usually protected by high walls and gates, which are for privacy as much as security.

IN THE VILLAGE

The pace and nature of life in a village is very different. With the migration to cities, a far smaller proportion of the population lives in the village than was the case fifty years ago. Four generations of one family may live under the same roof in a village, with people perhaps

just sleeping on the floor. In some of the best-situated villages, city dwellers have started buying up the available property. Indeed, it seems that much of north Tehran decamps each spring and summer vacation to newly built villas in villages in the north close to the Caspian Sea.

Few Iranian films evoke the atmosphere of an Iranian village as well as Darioush Mehrjui's 1969 masterpiece, *The Cow (Ghaav)*. The story of a simple village man whose dearest love is his cow—whose disappearance causes him to go mad—the film is an extraordinary document of a way of life that has now become increasingly rare.

POPULATION EXPLOSION

The population explosion over the last half century and the movement of people from villages to towns is one of the most significant developments in modern Iranian history. Iran's population at the start of the 1970s was less than

30 million; now it is around 80 million. Forty years ago, the majority of people lived agrarian lives that saw them tied to their land and villages. But in recent years there has been a huge influx into the cities, especially Tehran. These demographic changes have had a massive impact on the country's social fabric, creating a huge and often poor urban population. Millions of people from the *shahrestan* have come to Tehran in search of the work and money they cannot find at home. The population growth has stabilized, due largely to a change of heart by the authorities in the 1990s to actively promote birth-control methods such as condoms and the pill in a family planning drive that won praise from international organizations. But this now may be changing (see below).

MARRIAGE AND SEXUAL RELATIONSHIPS
Marriage

Marriage is the key event in the life of an Iranian. Iran, especially Tehran, can seem liberal compared to many Middle Eastern societies but this does not alter the fact that premarital sexual relations are banned by law and frowned upon by society. In today's tough economic times, it is also often only through marriage that young people can find the money to buy a house. As a result, Iranians tend to marry young. Many are shocked by foreigners who are still single in their thirties—in Iran this would be seen as either a calamity or an act of social defiance. The unmarried should be prepared to expect a barrage of fascinated questions—"*Chera ezdevaj nakardid? Dir shod!*" (Why aren't you married yet? It's getting late!) Many Iranians marry in their early twenties and as the thirties approach, particularly for women, society regards them as moving past their sell-by date. But while this is the rule, it should be noted that as ever in this country there are always exceptions.

The act of choosing a spouse is also very different from in the West. In most families, it will be the parents, in particular the mother, who makes the final decision and perhaps even the selection of a spouse. Marrying in defiance of one's mother is seen as the ultimate act of anti-parental rebellion, although it does happen. Female virginity is usually considered an essential precondition for marriage.

Weddings themselves are usually the most spectacular event in an Iranian's social calendar. A gargantuan feast is prepared, with those wonderful, sophisticated dishes that feature large in Iranian cookery books but are nonexistent in restaurants. Everyone dresses up—as mentioned previously, men will often sport a tie for wedding celebrations even if they do not at any other time. The bridal dress is usually expensive and elaborate—little different, if at all, from the dresses worn by brides in the West. For the more liberal families, a wedding celebration is also a rare chance for music and dancing with friends in a public space without the threat of a police warning.

The bridal car will be topped off with a huge ribbon and flowers and likely driven up urban highways at an even more extreme speed than usual. The Iranian obsession with the video camera (no one who can afford one seems to be without it, or to leave it out of their pocket for an instant) is even more in evidence. One of the most bizarre sights of a wedding day is the cameraman leaning precariously with most of his torso out of a speeding car on a highway in order to obtain the best possible shots of the bridal vehicle with his video camera.

Temporary Marriage (*Sigheh*)

Uniquely in Islam, Shiite Islam offers the possibility of a temporary marriage, known in Persian as *sigheh*. It is sometimes known as a "pleasure marriage," which is a fair description of its purpose. In *sigheh*, a man and woman can agree to be legally married for a limited period lasting as little as an hour. The idea is seen by its defenders as a way for genuine sexual needs to be fulfilled in a legal and proper way. Critics see it as little more than organized prostitution. In any case, temporary marriage is still not a widespread phenomenon in Iran (although certainly it is used) and it is not a concept that outsiders should raise without care. In theory, a man could take a second wife under a temporary marriage alongside his first lawful wife. But although polygamy is theoretically possible in Iran, in reality it is rare.

Family Planning

In the years immediately after the Revolution, families were officially encouraged to have as many children as possible. The idea was to create thousands of new "little revolutionaries" who would make Iran an even more powerful country in the future. It was also seen as necessary to counter the horrifying losses of the eight-year war with Iraq. By and large people responded, resulting in a population explosion in the 1980s. But it then became clear that the economy could not sustain such a huge youth population, which was starting to suffer chronic unemployment. The Rafsanjani presidency reversed the policy, and encouraged families to have only two children The plan has been a great success, with the birth rate falling from seven births per woman in 1980 to less than two now. Foreign visitors to Iran have often been stunned by the wide availability of condoms in pharmacies and the easy purchase of the pill over the counter. Iranian factories meanwhile produce homegrown condom brands.

But concerned by declining population growth, the authorities appear to have changed tack again, particularly after a 2012 speech by Khamenei that condemned the policies encouraging birth control. Many in Iran think driving the population over 150 million will ensure its future status as the regional superpower. State publicity campaigns are again promoting large families, with slogans like "More Children for a Happier Life." Funding for the state-run family planning program has been cut. There have been plans in parliament to pass legislation to outlaw voluntary sterilization and limit access to contraception.

Abortion is banned in Iran, with the only exceptions allowed when the woman's life is proven to be in danger. Attitudes toward sex are, of course, colored by the official ban on premarital sexual relations and the importance of virginity. Some Iranian youths appear very repressed. There is an unsettling black-market trade in home videos of women in private situations, such as dressing or swimming.

Homosexuality

Homosexuality is strictly illegal in Iran. Surprisingly, sex-change operations are not and the state can even provide funding for people who want to change their sex. Permission for sex-change operations came in a *fatwa* from Ayatollah Khomeini himself. The state sees transsexuals as sick and in need of medical help. As a result, Iran carries out more sex-change operations than any other country in the world after Thailand.

The degree to which homosexuals are repressed in Iran is a matter of huge controversy abroad. President Ahmadinejad caused astonishment when he once declared there were "no homosexuals" in Iran; it does not take too much probing to discover a very discreet underground culture.

CHILDHOOD

Iranians love to indulge children (*bache*). The approach toward parenting seems a little more permissive than in the West and children are positively encouraged to jump around and make noise. Western residents walking their children in Tehran parks often find their offspring the subject of the most lavish praise from passers-by, who think nothing of stroking, squeezing, or touching the child to show their goodwill. They will often use *Mashallah*, an Arabic phrase that is invoked when praising something beautiful to emphasize that it comes from God and thus avoid inviting the dangers of the "evil eye."

EDUCATION

Schooling starts from age six with five years of elementary school, then three years at junior high school, and three years at high school. Competition for places at the best universities is ferocious, although in recent years the creation of private universities has greatly increased the number of places available.

The standard of teaching is high. But a degree is no guarantee of finding a good job and it is not hard to find over-qualified young people delivering pizzas or driving taxis. There has been a substantial brain drain to countries such as Canada that take advantage of the excellent education of Iranians.

The lack of employment opportunities also puts a strain on parents, who may have to work extra hours in order to see their children through university.

For young men, military service of around two years is obligatory from the age of eighteen—how long depends on the hardship or ease of the service.

APPEARANCE AND PLASTIC SURGERY

Iran's youth, both male and female, take great care of their appearance. Many young men would not think of stepping out without sporting carefully gelled and styled hair, and with some women the same is true for makeup. One surprise for visitors to urban Iran is the number of young people walking around with plasters stuck across their noses. The explanation: there is a tremendous fashion for nose jobs (*damagh amali*), especially among women but also among men, and across all social classes.

chapter six

TIME OUT

Given the amount of traffic on weekend nights in Tehran, it seems that everyone is up to something. Iranians take their leisure seriously, and have a reasonable amount of time to enjoy it in. The weekend in Iran is Thursday and Friday: everyone has Friday off and most offices are shut on Thursdays as well. People also have a fair amount of holiday time thanks to the lengthy break for Nowruz and, as we have seen, the number of national holidays in the country.

In general, Iranians enjoy being together in groups. As in many Middle Eastern countries, there is a fear of being alone and being seen to be alone. Iranians are a gregarious people and whether hiking up a mountain or enjoying a kebab in a restaurant, they like to be part of a large group.

Unsurprisingly in this diverse country, the manner in which people enjoy their leisure varies considerably. Before the Revolution, Tehran was seen as the playground of the Middle East, complete with casinos and cabarets. These have now gone, and people focus their social lives on parties and dinners in private homes. The complexity of Iranian dishes means that cooking can easily fill a lot of free time. Soccer is a national obsession, although other sports are also popular.

EATING

Iranian food is acknowledged as one of the great cuisines of the world and Iranians are justly proud of it. But as in many countries, the best place to sample real Iranian food is at a private home and not in a restaurant. Often it is only in a house that visitors will be able to enjoy the full range of regional and national dishes and understand the elaborate culture behind them.

Eating at Home
Starters

An Iranian meal is likely to start with *sabzi* (herbs), fresh herbs possibly with walnuts, and feta cheese with bread. Eating the herbs is said to build up your appetite for the meal ahead.

A standard soup is *soup-e jo*, barley soup. There is also a thick meat soup known as *ash*, which is popular for breaking the Ramazan fast but simply too heavy and rich to be considered a starter. Another popular starter is the attractively named *koukou*, an omelet with a passing resemblance to a Spanish tortilla that is often served cold. Olives (*zeytun*) may also be served but do not expect the endless Arab-style sequence of *mezze* starters, which are not really part of Iranian cuisine.

Main Dishes

The main meal is likely to include delicious kebabs with rice, the standard Iranian dish. Forget the slices of indefinable meat served up after a late night out in the West: Iranian kebabs are the real thing, meat cooked on skewers over a charcoal fire. Often they will be cooked in the open over a barbecue—this is the one time an Iranian man can be seen helping out with cooking, sweating as he fans the coals. There are many kinds of kebabs—the most basic is *kubide* (minced), *juje* is chicken, while the best of all is *barg* (lamb). These are always served with rice (*berenj*). Iranians are justifiably proud of their rice, which is always of the Basmati kind. It is cooked and sifted several times so the final product is steaming hot and feather light. It will be topped off

by a circle of saffron-colored rice and butter. Many Iranians will munch their way through an entire raw onion while eating their meat. Rice is often served with barberries (*zereshk*), which provide a beautiful sweet-sour taste.

The meal will also include beef or lamb stews (*khoresht*), the jewels of Iranian cuisine and the perfect complement to the rice. Traditional stews include *gheimeh bademjoun* (eggplant stew) and *ghormeh sabzi*, which is made with several different herbs. But the greatest of them all is *fesenjun*, a rich and

original creation made with chicken, pomegranates, and walnuts. Other delicacies are *kofte tabrizi*, gigantic tennis-ball-sized meatballs from the north of Iran often stuffed with dates and served in a rich sauce. *Khashke bademjoun* is a smoky eggplant puree.

As elsewhere in the Middle East, stuffed vegetables (*dolme*) are also popular.

A feature of Iranian cuisine from medieval times to the present day is the use of sweet ingredients such as apricots, berries, oranges, and apples in savory main dishes. Perhaps the greatest Iranian dish of all is jeweled rice (*morasa polo*), which is served with carrots, crystallized sugar, saffron, orange, and dried fruit. This dish, which looks as extraordinary as it tastes, is nowadays only brought out on the most special occasions such as weddings.

Dessert

After all this, you may not have enough room for dessert, which normally includes Iranian cakes and cookies. The former can be a bit too creamy for some Western tastes—although slim locals seem to gorge themselves endlessly. The cookies are delicious, often flavored with saffron and varying greatly from region to region.

It is now time to thank your host—Iranian cuisine is time-consuming and elaborate. Even preparing the rice to ensure it has just the correct light texture can take hours. For a major feast, the host may have been preparing the dishes for days.

Eating Out
Restaurants

Most Iranians rarely step inside a restaurant, the idea being why pay for something you can get free and better at home! Often, an Iranian restaurant will offer only a limited selection of dishes, most likely kebabs. Standards of hygiene are generally good and the quality is fine, but an endless diet of kebabs can become quite dull. However, a much more interesting gastronomic culture is starting to take root in Tehran, with restaurants appearing that have become must-visit places for the fashionable youth. Iranian food is rarely expensive: a plate of kebabs and rice usually costs little more than US $5.

In Tehran, international food is increasingly popular with the moneyed elite. There are several good Indian, Chinese, Italian, Lebanese, and French restaurants. However, they are often hidden in the basements of hotels or shopping centers and are hard to find at random. A three-course international meal in

Tehran with (soft) drinks is likely to cost around US $20 per person.

Fast Food

Cheaper ideas include the increasingly ubiquitous fast-food restaurants, which are a known haunt of flirting couples, who seem attracted more by the social interaction than the often uninspired food. Nevertheless the atmosphere is extremely friendly and the burgers and pizzas pass muster in an Iranian kind of way. The Tehran equivalent of McDonald's is the amusingly named Boof, which is constantly opening new outlets. Fast food in Iran, however, may not be that fast—you line up to place an order, pay, and are then given a number that is finally read out over a microphone when the food is ready. Another option is the traditional kebab house, where the meat is excellent and is eaten with fresh round *taftoon* bread baked on the premises. A plate of kebabs and fresh herbs here can cost as little as US $3.

BREAD

Iranian bread is unique to the country—it is simply not possible to find the same kinds of bread anywhere else in the world. Iranians take bread very seriously and will refuse to eat it when it is not fresh.

There are four main types of bread in Iran and plenty of debate among Iranians over which is best. Bread generally acts as a culinary hoover—it is used to scoop up meat, cheese, and salad in morsel packages. Part of the fun is buying it. Bread shops sell only one of the four main types: for a different bread you have to go to a different shop. All bread is sold fresh from the oven; storekeepers would not sell anything else. In any case, if you wait too long before eating the bread or storing it, it becomes so crisp as to be inedible. Bakers usually only bake at mealtimes, three times a day, and there are long lines as breakfast, lunch, or dinner approaches. This is because subsidies mean that bread is kept cheap and it is the main carbohydrate for the poor. Despite the frustrations of standing in line, catching the whiff of the freshly baked bread early on a crisp sunny morning is one of the great simple pleasures of Iran.

In Tehran and other big cities, it is also possible to find shops making European-style bread and baguettes.

The four main types of bread are as follows:

Lavash: The most basic bread, ultra-thin layers used for scooping up food. A family will need to buy a dozen layers for a meal. It is seen by some as the poor man's bread.

Taftoon: An oval or round bread the size of a tray. Baking in a hot oven produces its characteristic air bubble dimples. It is especially good for eating with kebabs and best eaten hot.

Babari: An oblong-shaped bread with a doughy crust and a crispy inside, often topped with sesame seeds. It is very tasty with herbs or cheese.

Sangak: The undisputed king of Iranian breads, this is a long sheet of bread of medium thickness cooked over stones or pebbles (hence its name: *sang* means stone). Lines for this bread are always the longest. It is bliss if eaten fresh but has the texture of an old carpet if stale. Watch out for any lingering small stones remaining inside the bread, but at least they prove it's genuine!

For a breakfast out, a dubious delicacy is the *kalleh pacheh* (head and legs of a sheep). The restaurants offering this are clean, cheap, and friendly. They normally also bake *taftoon* on the premises. But the food—sheep's eyes, tongue, stomach, head, legs, and whatever else—served with a bowl of the cooking juices may not be to everyone's taste.

"Hot" and "Cold" Food

In another legacy of ancient times, the idea of "hot" (*garm*) and "cold" (*sard*) foods remains important in Iranian cooking today. This does not refer to the temperature of the food but to its influence on the mood and digestion. Iranians are convinced of the importance of having a good balance between "hot" and "cold" foods. The notion goes back to ancient Greek and Zoroastrian medicine, where it was believed that excessive "hot" food could make people hyperactive and feverish while too much "cold" food would lead to shivering and depression. Conversely, "hot" or "cold" foods could be prescribed to correct a range of ills.

The classification of hot and cold foods can seem confusing to outsiders. But generally, "hot" foods include the most widely eaten meats in Iran (lamb and chicken) and some spices, while "cold" foods include yogurt, rice, and most vegetables. Thus "hot" meat is balanced with "cold" rice and perhaps yogurt. Many Iranians remain passionately convinced of the importance of balancing the two kinds of foods, to ensure the taste is good, the digestion is smooth, and the mood temperate. They will warn of the dangers of having the wrong balance and also use the system to cure illness.

DRINKING

Alcohol is banned in Iran, but there are plenty of other options. Beer *is* available, but of course it is zero percent. The most popular Iranian brand is Delster, which is flavored with apple or lemon and is extremely refreshing on a hot day. Some would say it tastes absolutely nothing like beer. For a more beery taste, opt for imported foreign brands like Tuborg, Bavaria, and Baltika, which have good-quality zero percent options. Visitors should not be excited by mentions of "champagne" on upscale hotel menus as this will be sparkling grape juice. It is of course possible to source alcohol on the black market— smuggled in through Iraqi Kurdistan or Turkey.

Iranians are obsessive tea drinkers. The traditional way to drink tea in Iran is through a piece (*ghand*) of sugar clenched between the teeth, complete with a loud sucking noise—not for those who care for their dental health. Many Iranians take their first sips of tea by pouring the liquid into a saucer and then tipping it into their mouth. Tea is always served very strong and will taste very bitter without sugar. If you want a weak cup, ask for *kam-e rang* (literally, little color). Don't think of asking for milk except in five-star hotels—the locals will think you have lost your mind.

Coffee has traditionally not been massively popular but this is now starting to change, especially in Tehran, as European-style coffee shops draw the crowds and have become popular meeting places. Often tiny and extremely intimate establishments, they sell real coffee and cakes This is where the trendy set is likely to hang out, hunched over tables in deep and hushed conversation with their partners. Indeed, going to such a coffee shop will be the focal point of a night out for many young people in Iran.

There are traditional tea houses (confusingly named *ghavekhune*, coffeehouse), where you can lounge on a divan smoking a water pipe. Such places are often wonderfully atmospheric and a good place to chat with the older generation.

TIPPING

Tipping is nowhere near as widespread in Iran as in some other countries in the region. For short taxi journeys, cheaper restaurants, or hotels, tipping is absolutely not required unless you want to show great personal appreciation. In smarter restaurants, there may be a doorman to usher you in who will expect to be tipped half a dollar or so.

The main season for tipping comes just ahead of the New Year, when it is customary to give employees or workers an *eidi* (festive gift). For workers in companies, this normally means a salary for a thirteenth month. But house cleaners, drivers, or cooks will also expect to be paid the equivalent of an extra month's wage as well.

PAYING

Iran's economy runs on cash. The US trade embargo and international sanctions mean that international credit cards and traveler's checks from any company are next to useless here. The step-by-step removal of sanctions expected from 2016 under the 2015 nuclear deal should, if all goes to plan, eventually transform the Iranian economy's interaction with the outside world. But for now the vast majority of transactions, even for high-denomination goods, are made in cash.

Until as recently as 2005, the only note of real value was the 10,000 rial (known as a *sabzi*, or "green," because of its color, and worth now only about US $0.3), meaning that many payments involved handing over huge bricks of cash. Things improved with the introduction of 20,000- and 50,000-rial notes, the latter bearing a motif in support of the Iranian nuclear program, and now there is also a top value 100,000 rial note. With the economy hitting tough times due to sanctions, inflation has soared and the currency's value has been battered. Whereas there were 10,000 rials to the dollar in 2008, a single greenback is now worth 30,000 rials.

Another alternative are "Iran checks," essentially a domestic traveler's check issued by the central bank in denominations of 500,000 rials and one million rials. They are an alternative to avoid carrying heavy wads of notes. Using an international credit card is next to impossible in Iran, with the country cut off from international payment systems due to the sanctions. However, given the political context the situation is likely to change rapidly. Iranians are also increasingly using debit cards tied to an Iranian bank account, and pre-paid debit cards are also a practical option.

Toman or Rial?

In Iran, things are not always what they seem at first and, confusingly, this is the case with money. The national currency is the rial. The snag is that almost everyone, from financial bosses to shopkeepers, talks about money in terms of "tomans," which is the same as the rial but with one zero lopped off. So 10,000 rials is the same as 1,000 tomans, and if a taxi driver asks you for "5,000" at the end of a ride, he means he wants 5,000 tomans and thus 50,000 rials. The confusion means that most foreigners will end up underpaying by a factor of 10 at some point in their visit—but of course the Iranian vendor can be counted on to point out the error, as always in the most polite way possible!

SPORTS
Watching and Supporting
Soccer
Like almost everywhere else in the world, soccer (*footbol*) is the number one spectator sport with Iranians. Expect most men and quite a large number of women to be watching their televisions or at least listening

to the radio each time the national side plays an important match, with fervent celebrations of car-honking and flag-waving greeting a victory. Without ever setting the world on fire, Iran's national football team has had a steady record of success, qualifying for the World Cup Finals in 1978, 1998, 2006, and 2014. Its finest hour was at the 1998 tournament in France when the team beat the United States 2–1 in a match played in tremendous spirit that sent a strong signal for reconciliation.

Since 2011, Iran's football team has been coached by the Portuguese former Real Madrid manager and ex-assistant to Alex Ferguson at Manchester United, Carlos Queiroz. He has presided over a policy of inviting more players from the Iranian diaspora such as US-born Steven Beitashour. Only a late Lionel Messi goal destroyed Iran's hopes of qualifying for the knockout rounds of the 2014 World Cup in Brazil in a gutsy 0–1 defeat to Argentina. The team now plays with an image of the Asiatic Cheetah—one of the country's most emblematic and endangered animals—on their jerseys, earning them the nickname "the Persian cheetahs."

Just as apparent is the fervent support for local clubs. Tehran supporters are split down the middle over their devotion to either of the capital's two top teams—Persepolis (named after the famed ancient site in the south) and Esteghlal (Independence). Local derbies are massive events, with around 100,000 people packed into the Azadi (Freedom) Stadium in Tehran. The atmosphere is intimidating and the noise overwhelming—an extraordinary Iranian experience. The city for once becomes eerily quiet when the two teams play as Tehranis cluster in front of their television and radio sets.

Other Sports
Wrestling has a big following in the country and Iran has provided many Olympic and world champions. Basketball is also a major spectator sport and players have even been shipped in from the United States to play in the Iranian league. Handball is also popular with spectators, while the success of the men's volleyball team at an international level has won it many supporters.

Women in Sports
Women are increasingly well catered to in sports in Iran. In the years immediately after the Islamic Revolution, women's sports were frowned upon, but since the early 1990s the situation has improved considerably. Faezeh, the daughter of the then President Rafsanjani, was herself a keen sportswoman and fought hard for greater sporting opportunities for women. Initially, women were only encouraged to take part in more stationary activities like shooting and archery. But with time, they are now able to enjoy a full range of sports including highly physical activities like rowing, karate, canoeing, tennis, and even rugby. One thing that has not changed, however, is sexual segregation—women and men have to work out at different times at sports clubs. It would be inconceivable for women and men to compete together in any kind of sport, in public at least. Women also have to adhere fully to the Islamic dress code if they are playing sports while male spectators, coaches, or referees are in attendance.

In a hugely controversial measure, women have been banned from attending football matches in Iran since the Revolution. The authorities claim this is to protect them from male fans. Jafar Panahi's 2006 film *Offside* explores the adventures of women trying to attend a 2006 World Cup qualifying match in disguise with touching comedy and pathos. Despite occasional indications the ban could be lifted and a genuine public debate on the issue, it remains in force.

In 2012, the ban was extended to cover matches in volleyball, a hugely popular indoor sport in Iran. In an episode that received wide international coverage, a young British Iranian woman, Ghoncheh Ghavami, was arrested in June 2014 for attending a protest outside a volleyball stadium calling for women to be allowed to watch an international match. She was sentenced to one year in prison but then released on bail in November and pardoned in late March 2015.

Despite this, there is no restriction on women participating in most sports, although they must abide by the Islamic dress rules, which means no shorts and obliges some kind of headdress. Iranian sportswomen have notched up successes in sports ranging from athletics to football to rowing at an Asian level, although an Olympic breakthrough may still be some way off. In a sign of the obstacles faced by women, in 2015 the captain of the Iranian women's soccer team, Niloufar Ardalan, was reportedly prevented from traveling to an indoor championship by her husband who did not give permission to renew her passport in time. She was, however, allowed to leave for the next competition abroad after the judiciary overruled him.

Zurkhaneh

Perhaps Iran's most intriguing sport for foreign spectators is *Zurkhaneh* (House of Strength). The sport consists of several disciplines, including traditional wrestling, lifting clubs and shields, and spinning in a circle at a dizzying speed. This spellbinding combination of wrestling, weightlifting, and traditional strongman events is accompanied by traditional music and provides one of the best possible insights into the Iranian psyche. There are clubs in most Iranian cities:

they can be found by asking around and visitors are usually welcome. The sport is also known as *varzesh-e bastani* (ancient sport) and Iranians are proud that its origins go back to the pre-Islamic period. Today, of course, religious devotion also plays its role in the sport, with the players calling on the prophets before performing their disciplines.

Taking Part

It is surprisingly easy to find sporting activities in Iran. Almost everything is available—even darts and cricket—and the standard of facilities is good. Ask an Iranian to phone the appropriate sports federation for more information.

Park Sports

Among people in search of less formal sporting activities, badminton is all the rage. Go to any park on a Friday or a summer evening and all the open spaces will be crammed with people, men and women, pinging a shuttlecock back and forth. If you bring along a racket, you are bound to be asked to join in—a great way to make new friends. There is also plenty of informal park volleyball, although this probably requires some previous experience and skill to be truly satisfying.

Mountain Sports

Another active pursuit popular all over Iran (for both sexes) is hiking. Iran is the most mountainous country in the Middle East and in no other country in the region is hiking so popular. Iran has produced some world-class mountaineers who have climbed all the world's major peaks. There are also excellent bolted climbing routes within easy reach of Tehran

and other cities. But mountain walking is also
extremely popular with the public—every Friday,
the main mountain trails above Tehran are packed
with locals enjoying the better air and weekend
exercise. People come from all social backgrounds—
fit septuagenarians, *chador*-clad women, and young
children bound up the hills—perhaps the only
chance they have all week for activity and decent air.
The sound of a man singing poetry as he ascends
a mountain is another of those unique Iranian
experiences. The trails are so busy on a Friday that
the walking can be a bit stressful and it might be
better to choose any other day in the week.

With the help of a guide, visitors can find
plenty of great treks in the Alborz Mountains
around Tehran or in the Zagros Range to the
west. The country as a whole has a huge choice
of mountain landscapes largely unexplored
by foreigners. Any mountaineer in Iran wants
to ascend its highest peak, Mount Damavand.
Although close to Tehran, a guided climb to the

summit and back takes the best part of a week—a feat well within the reach of a fit walker in summer, although best left to alpine specialists in the winter.

CULTURE
Cinema

Iranian cinema is rightly famed worldwide for its quality and has a proud tradition dating back to well before the Islamic Revolution to the dawn of the medium. The first Iranian feature film is generally reckoned to be *Abi and Rabi* by the Iranian Armenian Ovanes Ohanian, from 1930. Many Iranian films have won top prizes at international film festivals in recent years. *The Taste of Cherry* (*Ta'm-e Gilas*, 1997), directed by Abbas Kiarostami, about a man trying to commit suicide in Tehran, won the Palme d'Or in Cannes and caused much controversy back home for its subject matter. *The Circle* (*Dayereh*, 2000) by Jafar Panahi, a gritty look at the problems of a group of women in Tehran, took top prize at the Venice Film Festival. But directors and their actors have also had to battle sometimes crippling censorship that has caused them to leave the country or even face prosecution. The restrictions on sensitive political and religious subject matter became tighter after the 2009 protests, which many prominent artists supported.

But Iranian filmmakers have kept notching up successes against the odds. Asghar Farhadi's lacerating study of an Iranian couple in the throes of divorce, *A Separation* (*Jodai-ye Nader az Simin*), won best foreign-language film at the Oscars in 2012. As well as exposing the agony of a disintegrating relationship, the film is also a remarkably authentic portrayal of contemporary Iranian society. Farhadi has always had a delicate dance with the censors in Iran and tellingly his next film, *The Past*, was made in France.

Meanwhile the legendary Kiarostami, apparently tired of his brushes with the censors, began making films only outside Iran. One of its best known actresses, Golshifteh Farahani, left the country permanently after coming under fire from hardliners for starring in an American movie alongside Leonardo DiCaprio.

But no-one illustrates the resourcefulness and sheer bravery of Iranian filmmakers better than Jafar Panahi. Feted worldwide for the *The Circle* in 2000 and *Offside* in 2006, Panahi never relented in his ambition to make socially realistic and truthful cinema. A passionate supporter of the 2009 protests, Panahi was convicted in 2010 of spreading anti-government propaganda. He was sentenced to jail (although never sent to prison to serve his term), held under house arrest, and, most significantly, banned from filmmaking. But Panahi refused to be cowed, and with *This is Not a Film* (2011) wittily explored the absurdity of his own predicament. Famously, it was shown at the 2011 Cannes Film Festival after being smuggled out of Iran in a USB stick hidden inside a cake. Panahi went step further with *Taxi* (2015), where playing himself as a taxi driver he constructs a portrait of contemporary Tehran through the passengers he meets. The film won the prestigious Golden Bear at the Berlin film festival, where the head of the jury hailed it as a "love letter to cinema." With Panahi having no passport and banned from leaving Iran, the award was tearfully accepted by his young niece Hana Saeidi.

Whether this proud cinematic tradition means a visitor will ever go to the cinema in Iran is another matter. Rather than the art-house fare that is so successful in the West, many of the films screened in Iran tend to be macho shoot-em-ups or banal boy-meets-girl tales. Unsurprisingly, plenty of business is done in pirate DVDs, whose sellers will happily flog copies of otherwise banned material for little more than US $2. They ply their trade outdoors near major squares or in near-stationary traffic jams despite occasional police crackdowns.

Music
Traditional and Western Classical

Iran's music scene is also the subject of strict rules but is nevertheless surprisingly diverse. Traditional Iranian music normally involves a small group of instrumentalists accompanying a vocalist singing traditional poetry. The songs take their time to build up to an intense climax and are not really easy listening but can be a profoundly moving experience. The undisputed master of traditional Iranian singing is Mohammad Reza Shajarian, a household name in Iran, whose rare concerts both at home and abroad sell out almost instantly. He is known in Iran simply as *ostad*—the master.

The most common instruments are the *tar* (long-necked lute), the *kamancheh* (spike fiddle, played with a bow), the *ney* (flute), and the *tombak* (drum). Some traditional concerts take place in

Tehran, although not as many as people would like. Frustratingly, any advertising tends to be by word of mouth. A likely venue to ask is the cultural center of Niavaran Palace in northern Tehran. The atmosphere of Iranians enjoying the rare event of attending a concert can be electric.

Western classical music exists in Iran and Tehran has its own symphony orchestra, whose eclectic repertoire includes Mozart as well as Iranian and Eastern composers. Western classical music was frowned upon immediately after the Revolution (perhaps in response to its promotion by the deposed shah's wife), but the Tehran symphony orchestra has revived in recent years under its conductor Ali Rahbari. Famed conductor and pianist Daniel Barenboim even planned to take his Berlin orchestra to Tehran, but the idea hit opposition due to his Israeli citizenship.

Pop Music

Rock music exists in two forms—legal and illegal. Several pop bands operate freely with official permission from the Ministry of Culture and Islamic Guidance, which deems them to be acceptable. Iran's first aboveground post-revolution pop group was Arian, which gave its first public performance in 1998 after President Khatami came to power. It was also remarkable for having female backing vocalists and instrumentalists.

Only a few bands win the all-important official approval, leaving a substantial underground music scene. These can range from small-scale ensembles to something more serious, and any concerts they give can be subject to raids by the police. There is also a thriving Persian diaspora music scene based around Los Angeles—plenty of the music heard in Tehran traffic jams will have been produced in LA.

Art

Art galleries of modern works are surprisingly plentiful in Tehran and have a fashionable ambience. There are many talented Iranian artists—Kiarostami himself is one. Unbeknownst to many, Iran also has a spectacular collection of European art, including major works by Bacon, Picasso, Pollock, and Renoir. Built up under the deposed shah, it is now kept firmly under lock and key in Tehran's Museum of Contemporary Art and shown only to specialist visitors. Under Khatami, a large chunk was shown to the public briefly for the first time since the Revolution.

chapter seven

TRAVEL, HEALTH, & SAFETY

Traveling to and within Iran is in the throes of momentous change following the 2015 deal on the Iranian nuclear program. Visiting is becoming easier, more accessible, and safer than ever since the Islamic Revolution. Whereas Iran has been seen as one of the world's most closed countries, it is now, for the first time in years, actively encouraging foreign tourists to visit. Iranian officials have predicted a "tsunami" of tourists who will come and enjoy the country's nineteen UNESCO-listed world heritage sites. The lifting of sanctions means that hotel and aviation infrastructure should finally improve. But with officials seeking to quadruple current tourist arrivals of some four million a year, it remains to be seen if the infrastructure can keep up with the increase in visitor numbers.

VISAS

Obtaining a visa for Iran used to be a tricky and often hit-and-miss business, with applications rejected for no obvious reason. But with the authorities finally understanding the huge boost tourism can give to the struggling economy, this is now changing. From 2015, the Iranian authorities have started issuing 30 day visas—with the

possibility of a 15 day extension—at Tehran airport
for citizens of dozens of EU, Middle Eastern, Asia–
Pacific, and Latin American countries. Meanwhile,
travel Web sites have emerged that greatly facilitate
the process of obtaining a visa from an Iranian
embassy. The airport visa scheme includes most
EU states. But it notably excludes Britain, Canada,
and the United States, meaning the citizens of those
countries will still need to obtain visas from Iranian
diplomatic representations. The reopening of Iran's
embassy in Britain in August 2015—the same time
as the reopening of the British embassy in Tehran
after the 2011 ransacking—eases this for British
citizens. Britain's Foreign Office warns that British
citizens may also face problems obtaining visas from
online agencies. It is still, in theory, possible to visit
the free trade zone of Iran's Kish Island for 14 days
without a visa.

ARRIVING IN IRAN
Air Travel

Virtually all international flights for Tehran leave
from and land at the Imam Khomeini International
Airport (IKIA). The airport has had a difficult
history—when it first opened it was shunned by
many airlines amid concerns about the runway
safety. It was also stormed by the Revolutionary
Guards and closed down just hours after opening
in May 2004 on "security" grounds, but actually to
prevent a Turkish firm operating the airport. It is
now run by an Iranian state-owned operator. But
using the shiny IKIA is now a relatively pleasant
experience. It is also one of the few places in Tehran
where it is possible to buy a proper espresso. The

concourse is always crammed—whenever an Iranian goes abroad for any period of time, the whole family usually shows up for what is often an emotional farewell. The same goes for the homecoming, complete with tears and flowers.

The main problem with IKIA is its distance from Tehran—stuck out in the desert, it is a 30 mile (50 km) drive and takes an hour even in the traffic-free dead of night. There is usually a good supply of taxis that will be only too happy to oblige the disembarking foreigner. A frequent bus service during daytime hours connects with the metro system. One day, metro Line 1 will eventually be extended as far south as the airport, whisking travelers traffic free from the airport to Tajrish Square without changing.

Amid the tensions of the last years, several foreign airlines suspended their services to Tehran as passenger numbers plummeted, including Air France–KLM and British Airways. However these will resume as business picks up with the lifting of sanctions. In any case, connections are always possible with Iran Air or via Istanbul with Turkish Airlines, or with Arabian peninsula carriers.

Domestic flights meanwhile continue to be from Mehrabad airport, far closer to the center of the city. This airport used to be Tehran's airport before the opening of IKIA, but now has virtually no international flights.

INTERCITY TRAVEL
Bus and Taxi

Traveling by bus in Iran is normally a relatively comfortable experience, although not as leisurely as that in neighboring Turkey. The distances are in any case often very long (for example, around 18 hours from Tehran to Kerman) and in many cases it is better to take the plane. The best buses tend to be new Volvos or Scanias, while Mercedes models seem to have emerged from a 1960s time warp and are far less comfortable. It is always worth checking which make of bus is departing before booking the ticket. Bus stations, especially in Tehran, tend to be places of organized chaos, which seem intimidating at first but generally work efficiently. There are very many bus companies, but just asking around at the bus station will lead you rapidly toward the firm with the first bus leaving for your destination. Ticket prices are extremely low. A Western man should not sit next to an unmarried Iranian woman, but no one will ask Western couples whether they are married. Drivers are generally professional and on the better class of services you will be offered soft drinks and snacks en route.

However, Iran has one of the world's very worst safety records on its roads, which claim around four thousand lives a year. The reason is partly the erratic driving of many Iranians, in particular the drivers of heavy goods vehicles, some of whom are suffering from extreme exhaustion or even under the influence of drugs. Each year there are several horrific crashes involving buses, usually at night.

Travelers in southeast Iran are well advised to keep a close eye on their baggage: this is prime drug-smuggling territory and the police are likely to carry out spot checks on passing traffic.

For shorter journeys of up to three hours, shared taxis are usually available; they leave when full and charge a fixed fee. Journey times are shorter than for the bus, but stress levels will be higher as the drivers do not hang around.

Train

Iran's extensive train network is often overlooked by foreigners but it is perhaps the safest and most comfortable way to travel around the country. The expanding network has now extended to almost every major city in the country, and watching the mountains turn to desert outside your window is a thrilling experience. Most services originate in Tehran and are generally long distance, best suited to overnight journeys. In case of a delay of more than one hour, it is even possible to obtain a partial refund. The service is generally deemed to be excellent, but the snag is that demand outstrips supply, meaning that tickets need to be bought at least a week in advance and even more for the over-subscribed New Year period.

Having secured a ticket, you might find yourself on the nicely named Pardis (Paradise) higher-speed (160 km/hour) services from Tehran to Qom or Yazd, or an overnight sleeper to Tabriz or Shiraz. The ultimate in luxury is the new Zendegi train that circulates between Tehran and Mashhad and looks like something out of an Agatha Christie novel with its smartly dressed waiters. There is a project for a high speed (350 km/hour) link to Isfahan, while a luxury tourist train also takes travelers to Iran from Hungary via Turkey.

Air Travel

The aviation sector in Iran will be one of the most immediate and visible beneficiaries of the lifting of sanctions. US sanctions proscribed the sale of aircraft or parts to Iran, and even the servicing of parts. This forced the Iranian aviation industry into a variety of creative and sometimes shadowy practices in order to keep planes in the air. This explains the old age of the planes—two and a half decades old on average—serving routes inside Iran. For many, the aviation sanctions backfired: compromising the safety of Iranian citizens while doing nothing to enhance the image of the West in Iran.

A litany of air crashes raised serious questions over the safety of air travel in Iran among Iranians, foreign visitors, and even the government. Use of Russian-made aircraft had long sustained the industry in Iran, but in 2011 the government banned the use of the workhorse Tu-154 plane following the 2009 Caspian Airlines crash that killed 168 passengers and crew. The banning of the Tu-154 was a relief and a long overdue step for many Iranians who flew on the plane with trepidation over its twenty years of use in the country. Another deadly crash forced Iran to ground all flights of its home-built version of the Ukrainian An-140.

As a goodwill gesture, the United States in 2014 allowed Iran Air for the first time in years to buy spare parts. With the lifting of sanctions the industry will finally have full access to the global market and domestic air travel should be transformed. National flag carrier Iran Air, which in the 1970s was the fastest growing carrier in the world with a perfect safety record, will also benefit. Officials have said Iran wants to buy up to ninety aircraft a year from Boeing and Airbus to renew its fleet.

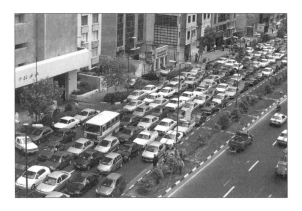

URBAN TRAVEL
Tehran Traffic

Traffic (*terrafik*) dominates almost every conversation in Tehran. It is not just bad, it is abominable, even by the standards of the Middle East. A poorly judged journey can result in being stuck in traffic snarls for literally hours, breathing in the polluted air as well. Tehran has an impressive network of four-lane highways, but even these are not enough to absorb the millions of cars on the city's roads. A liter of gasoline used to cost less than a liter of water under a heavy government subsidy program that kept drivers happy. But the subsidies have now been drastically scaled back as the authorities seek to shore up public finances, and a liter now retails for around US $0.36, over three times as much as half a decade ago.

Listening to radio traffic reports in the rush hour can be amusing, as the presenter announces that the traffic on almost every highway in the capital is *sangin* (heavy).

Pollution

The pollution (*aludegi*) in the city is generated almost entirely by the car exhaust fumes. Some say that living in the capital is the equivalent of smoking a dozen cigarettes a day. Tehran's attractive situation—at a high altitude and surrounded by mountains—is also its curse, especially in winter when huge amounts of smog build up in the city center. During the very worst periods—generally in winter after many days of no wind—the authorities even advise people to stay at home or shut down schools. Stuck in a traffic jam, the bitter smell of carbon monoxide is palpable. The sheer volume of traffic is not the only reason for this—the make of cars is also to blame. Until recently, the bulk of cars on Iranian roads were locally manufactured Paykans ("arrow" in Farsi), an extraordinarily inefficient vehicle that burns the same amount of fuel as a sports car, which was modeled on the British Hillman Hunter, a family car of the 1960s and '70s. Like an East German Trabant, the Paykan has a certain nostalgia value but its environmental impact has been catastrophic.

Iran has now finally stopped production of these cars in favor of more modern vehicles and the affluence of middle-class Tehranis means that there is a surprising number of smart new cars on the roads. But there are plenty of Paykans still around.

Coping with Tehran Traffic

The key to ensuring that traffic doesn't ruin your day's plans is good planning and timing. In Tehran, the traffic builds up from 7:00 a.m. as schools start and it reaches a crescendo at round 8:45 a.m. with commuters. Relative calm then prevails for a few hours, before school ends and the lunch break causes brief but extremely heavy traffic for an hour after midday. But the worst is yet to come: many employees seem to leave their work exactly at 5:00 p.m., resulting in horrendous problems from that time on. The main roads from Tehran city center to the richer residential areas in the north are filled with traffic until around 7:30 p.m., by which time it is normally safe to venture outside again.

Taxis

Most foreigners, and many Iranians, will use only taxis for their journeys in Tehran and other big cities. These will either normally be the Paykan or its more congenial replacement, the Samand. There are two types of taxi in Iran: a *savari* (shared) or a *dar bast* (literally, door closed). The former are basically shared cabs; as they come by the curb they honk and you yell your destination to the driver, who will either stop to take you or carry on driving if he is not interested. At busy times, dozens of Iranians stand at intersections waiting for *savari* taxis. The unspoken code was always that unrelated members of the opposite sex should avoid sitting next to each other, sometimes resulting in a roadside ballet as new passengers got in and the remaining ones changed their configuration. But things are more relaxed these days and the code is not always observed.

But given that the process of hailing a *savari* taxi can be daunting, many will prefer to pay extra for a private taxi, or *dar bast*. Essentially, any empty car can be taken this way so long as the driver agrees on the destination or price. For a journey from north to central Tehran the price is still low, at around US $6. Official taxis are marked by a horizontal stripe over the body of the car, although many taxis operate unofficially as well. The other option is to take a telephone taxi (*ajans*). There are usually several *ajans* offices in most neighborhoods in Iranian cities, providing an important source of income for men who would not otherwise find work. At busy times they may have no cars, but normally there is a decent supply.

Whatever kind of taxi you take, you may be in for an interesting experience: many of the older drivers are highly educated and opinionated and may even speak some English. With a younger driver, expect to be deafened by a succession of tracks of Iranian pop on the car stereo. Incongruously, some of the most beaten-up Paykans have been lovingly fitted out with state-of-the art stereos.

Metro

Tehan's rapidly expanding metro network has eased navigation of the traffic-clogged city, and with the recent opening of new stations become much more useful for tourists. Political upheaval meant construction of the Tehran metro started relatively late—the first plans were drawn up in 1971 with French contractors, but were shelved and only taken up again after the Islamic Revolution and the Iran–Iraq war. The first line was finally opened in 1999, and the metro currently has five lines, with two more under construction. In 2012, after years of delays, the metro's Line 1 finally reached the leafy northern Tehran neighborhood of Tajrish at the terminus of Vali Asr Street. It is now planned that Line 1 will reach as far south as IKIA airport. The expansion of the metro has helped ease the daily nightmare of commuting in Tehran a little, but will go much further with plans to increase the number of daily journeys from three million to nine.

Driving

Long-term foreign residents in Iran usually purchase a private car with good air-conditioning to avoid the pollution. However, it takes some time to adapt to the aggressive Iranian driving style. Indeed, what passes for cautious, sensible driving in the West can be dangerous in Tehran as no one expects people to drive like this. If you have an accident, you should not leave the scene until the police arrive. Iran is one of the few countries in the Middle East where the police actively enforce the law that seat belts must be worn in the front, and they will stop vehicles that disobey this on highways.

Pedestrians

For many visitors, traffic will be their most negative experience of Tehran. Perhaps the worst-off of all are pedestrians, who have to gulp in all the pollution and risk their lives when crossing the road. The sheer volume of traffic means pedestrians have to take one lane of cars at a time, often leaving them stranded in the middle of the road as vehicles zip by on each side. Iranians are in a hurry when they are in their cars, so do not expect the normal rules of hospitality toward foreigners to apply here.

A particular danger is the thousands of motorbikes that appear to hold the Tehran economy together by performing errands and deliveries. They can be found going the right way, going the wrong way, and on the sidewalk, and can zoom out of nowhere without the slightest warning. For the super brave, there is always the possibility of hailing one of these bikes as a taxi. Motorbike taxis weave in and out of the traffic so journey times are much shorter. But riding pillion behind a manic driver may not be to everyone's taste . . . though some foreigners may be happy to find it possible to have so much exhilaration so cheaply!

WHERE TO STAY

Hotels in Iran run from dormitories offering beds from a few dollars a night to multistar hotels where a night's rest can prove very expensive for foreigners. The increasing number of tourists visiting Iran is already causing problems with capacity at hotels, especially in the upscale sector. There is simply not enough supply to meet the expanding demand so it is essential to book ahead. Foreign firms are already waiting to dive back into the Iranian hospitality sector with the lifting of sanctions, and in October 2015 French hotel chain Accor opened hotels of both its Ibis and Novotel brands at IKIA airport. The move would have been unimaginable a few years before, but is likely only just the start. Arab chain Rotana is also set to open half a dozen luxury-end hotels in Tehran in the next years. Whether these openings in the capital— let alone outside Tehran— can keep pace with the expected dramatic increase in demand remains to be seen. At the lower end of the sector, things are more flexible and backpackers need not fret about finding a roof over their heads.

It is strictly illegal in Iran for unmarried men and women to share hotel rooms. The rule is easily enforced, as in Iran marriage is recorded in the passport. For Iranians there is no exception, although for non-Muslim foreigners the rules might be more relaxed.

HEALTH
Atmospheric Pollution
The fumes in Tehran are often the major health problem for visitors as well as Tehranis. It is not a good sign to see local residents going about their business wearing hygiene masks to avoid the pollution. Respiratory problems are widespread in Tehran, especially during the winter, and asthma sufferers have a particularly difficult time. Living in such a city is not easy and anecdotal evidence suggests a good number of residents visit a psychologist (*ravashenas*) to cope with the stress levels. Outside Tehran, pollution should not be an issue and the smaller Iranian cities have excellent air quality as they are often high up in the mountains.

Hygiene
Standards of hygiene in Iran are generally good, indeed far better than in many neighboring countries. Certainly, Tehran is a far cleaner city than Cairo, for example. Refuse collection is well organized and the streets are refreshingly free of litter for a Middle Eastern capital. Early risers in Tehran will be impressed by the sight of hundreds of municipal workers cleaning the city before dawn.

Restaurants and snack bars are generally clean and it would appear the health authorities keep a close eye to ensure basic standards of hygiene. Meat is normally very fresh, though it is worth ensuring it has been kept in a proper fridge during summer. Sometimes, in very hot periods, the authorities will ban restaurants from selling salads in some regions for public health reasons. It is worth being careful of the Iranian yogurt drink *doogh* in summer, as some shopkeepers keep their consignments in the sun outside.

Water is good to drink in almost all Iranian cities, especially in Tehran where it is said to come straight from the Alborz Mountains. However, many richer locals will only touch mineral water, which is cheaply and plentifully available in several different brands. There are a few places where the water is unsafe to drink, most notably the clerical city of Qom, where it has an uncomfortably high percentage of salt. People with sensitive stomachs would in any case feel happier drinking mineral water, given it is so cheap.

Public lavatories are not fantastic but bearable. As with all travel in this region, it is good to have liquid soap on hand for any bus journeys, during which the worst toilets are likely to be encountered. Generally, visitors can expect to leave Iran without having suffered any of the stomach problems that can bedevil visits to the Indian subcontinent.

Medical Treatment

The Iranian approach to using doctors and dentists is perhaps different from the West's. Few people in this quite fatalistic society bother with regular checkups. But if they do become sick, even with just a cold, they tend to go straight to a doctor. The idea of coping with a heavy cold simply by sitting at home and letting nature take its course is quite alien to Iranians. Doctors will often hand out prescriptions for a heavy quantity of medicines. They are also likely to offer the patient antibiotics, not only in the form of pills but as an injection. For many Iranians, it is quite normal to visit a doctor for an antibiotics injection as soon as they realize they are coming down with a cold.

Happily for this hypochondriac society, the medical profession is well trained and plentiful. If you fall ill there should be no problem finding a doctor's office or a medical practice. Standards of dental care are also very high. There are many pharmacies (*darookhune*), which always have a huge supply of medicine. Most medicines are generics and exceedingly cheap. You will probably be given a bottle of medicine or an envelope of tablets without any instructions about use, so it is worth asking the pharmacist about the frequency of the dose and any possible side effects.

SECURITY

Iran is indisputably one of the safest countries in the Middle East for travel—at least if the question of road safety is put aside. Muggings and thefts against foreigners are extremely rare. Women find they are confronted with far less hassle than in Egypt or Turkey. Security is good. While the early days of the Islamic Republic were marred by bomb attacks and assassination attempts by the outlawed opposition, today Iran appears to enjoy stability. Bomb attacks are nowadays almost unheard-of. Generally, foreign visitors end their trip to Iran without experiencing any problems and wonder why the country has such a poor reputation abroad.

Scams

As in all big cities, petty crime can be a problem. Here there are a small number of thieves with the usual gamut of tricks. Someone could pose as a policeman and demand your passport in a bid to steal it or extort a "fine." Never hand anything over, and either walk away or demand to be taken to a police station. Police normally go out of their way not to bother foreigners and it is almost inconceivable that a bona fide officer would ask for a tourist's documents in the street.

Also be aware of purse snatchers, who work at high speed from the back of motorbikes. Always make sure your backpack or camera bag is attached to both shoulders, so that it can't be pulled off.

High-Risk Regions

There are also a few isolated places where it is best not to venture, above all the southeastern Sistan–Baluchestan province that borders Afghanistan and Pakistan. Foreigners have been abducted in this area in recent years by criminal gangs involved in militant attacks and drug smuggling. In particular, avoid the road from Bam to Quetta in Pakistan via Zahedan, a known highway for drug trafficking and related kidnapping. Care should also be exercised in areas on the Iraqi and Turkish borders that have Arab or Kurdish ethnic-minority populations, which have been the scene of occasional separatist militant attacks. It also goes without saying not to photograph or venture near sensitive military, scientific facilities, let alone nuclear ones.

chapter eight

BUSINESS BRIEFING

Iran sits on the second-largest proven reserves of gas (some estimates say the biggest anywhere) and is a leading OPEC oil producer. It has many successful domestic firms with a long business tradition and one of the most highly educated workforces in the Middle East. Yet over recent years, the economy has been crippled by the sanctions imposed over its nuclear program. After the Joint Comprehensive Plan of Action (JCPOA) nuclear deal agreed between Iran and world powers in Vienna on July 14, 2015, the sanctions are being lifted and Iran looks set to become a fully functioning member of the world economy once again.

THE BUSINESS ENVIRONMENT
Sanctions and the Economy
Iran withstood years of US sanctions in the wake of the Islamic Revolution, but the measures were ramped up to a new intensity by the United States and the European Union in the standoff over its nuclear program. Oil output plummeted as customers scaled back or pulled out of purchases. The potential of the gas industry went untapped by foreign companies. The domestic banking industry was cut off from the international system. The partial lifting of

sanctions under the nuclear deal has changed this at a stroke. Under the terms of the deal, most regular international banking business with Iran is now possible and the import of Iranian energy supplies to Europe is no longer illegal.

This is having a huge impact on the hydrocarbon sector. Despite Iran's great gas reserves, growing domestic consumption and a lack of foreign investment has at times made it, astonishingly, a net importer of gas. Meanwhile, the sanctions forced a drop in output that saw Iran fall from being OPEC's number two to number five producer. Iranian energy officials are now predicting that billions of dollars of foreign investment will pour into the sector and are making ambitious projections about its export potential. EU firms are waiting to plunge back in, while European leaders hope Iran could reduce Europe's gas dependence on Russia.

Foreign Firms in Iran

First-time visitors have always been surprised by the amount of Western goods available in Iran, be it Tefal saucepans, Kellogg's cornflakes, or even Coca-Cola.

The cars of choice for middle-class Tehranis are likely to be Peugeots or Renaults—both mass-produced in the country in joint ventures with the national car firm Iran Khodro. But the sanctions saw a mass exodus of foreign companies and personnel from Tehran. Some did not shutter completely, shrewdly keeping offices open until business could resume. Foreign firms are now circling as the sanctions are lifted, sniffing out new contracts in anything from consumer goods to transport infrastructure. As when any emerging market opens up, a lot of money is to be made, and a lot of money is to be lost. In any case, Iran's full re-integration into the global economy is going to be a long road, rather than just a few years.

Under the sanctions regime, Iran's biggest trading partners were China, the United Arab Emirates, and Turkey, rather than the European Union. But this could change rapidly from 2016 with the resumption of energy exports to the West. The booming emirate of Dubai has become a crucial hub for Iranian business. Thousands of Iranian businessmen live there and Dubai links Iran to outside markets that would otherwise be cut off by the country's relative isolation.

Changing Money

Despite the political animosity, there is no problem exchanging US dollars. Euros are easy to change, pounds sterling a little less so outside Tehran. It's usually best to change money at a bureau de change—at banks the process and lines are likely to be long. In most cities money-changing offices are widespread, although in Tehran they are easiest to locate in the south of the city. Street changers also lurk outside and they are likely to offer a slightly better rate (though you should take extra care when handing over your dollars in the street).

THE ECONOMIC SITUATION

Inflation and Poverty

Despite the wealth of natural resources, the last years have been tough economically for Iran. Talking with ordinary people reveals that economic issues are by far their most pressing daily preoccupation. Young people may benefit from a good university education but there are often not the jobs to go around, and the result is very high youth unemployment. Prices have also surged in Iran in recent years and, while the cost of basic foodstuffs may still seem cheap compared to the West, they are very *gerun* (expensive) for poorer Iranians.

Many Iranians are convinced that all Westerners are fantastically rich, and given the meagerness of some incomes in the country they have a point. Many public-sector workers—in particular teachers, who are paid only a few hundred dollars a month—take second jobs as taxi drivers in the evenings in order to bring in sufficient money for their family. Some workers keep extremely low-paid day jobs (for example, as bus drivers) only because they offer certain social security benefits, and then try to earn some extra money in the evening in their taxis. The exhausting hours worked by many middle-aged men are a tribute to their industry and also their loyalty to their families. But foreign visitors should be tactful when discussing money matters, and to boast of a large salary or carelessly fiddle with a wad of notes could easily cause offense.

Privatization and State Control

The state retains control over around three-quarters of the economy: while there may seem to be a large number of different companies in various sectors, they are likely to be state-owned. Ayatollah Khamenei in 2006 ordered Iran's leaders to embark on a major privatization program that would affect 80 percent of state-owned companies. The only exceptions were in the energy and defense sectors. But real signs of progress in this domain have yet to be made. The Ahmadinejad government handed out a large number of shares in privatized companies as "justice shares" to the poor, rather than to investors. Private enterprise *does* exist in Iran, and sometimes with considerable success, but so far such firms are the exception and not the rule. There has also been talk of increasing foreign participation in the economy and state-owned enterprises, but again this has yet to be realized.

An important player in the economy is the elite ideological army, the Revolutionary Guards. Their economic contractors have in recent years won major contracts for extensions to the Tehran metro, gas pipelines, and other engineering projects. Critics have accused the Guards of profiting from the sanctions and for now restrictions on entities suspected of links to the Guards remain in place.

DOING BUSINESS IN IRAN
Business Meetings

When starting any business meeting, on no account expect to get to the point right away. The first minutes are a time for tea drinking and pleasantries about anything other than the matter in question. Indeed, it is quite normal for nothing much to happen in a first meeting, merely a breaking of the ice; the proper business will start at the next date. Iranian counterparts will show the utmost courtesy and a foreigner's standing will grow if this is displayed in return. Forms of address are important; US-style first-name terms have not yet hit the Iranian business scene. Men should be addressed as "*Agha-ye . . .*" (Mr. . . .) and women as "*Khanoom-e . . .*" (Ms. . . .). Academic qualifications are taken seriously in Iran and it is normal to call someone with a doctorate "*Agha-ye Doktor-e . . .*" (Mr. Doctor . . .). But affection is never far away, and it is also good form to use "*janam*" (literally, "my dear") before the terms of formal address. So if your main interlocutor is a Dr. Jaafari you could address him as "*Janam Agha-ye Doktor-e Jaafari.*"

Business cards will be exchanged. This is taken seriously by Iranians, but there is no ritual way of presenting them as in some Asian countries; the card needs simply to be handed over.

Dressing decently is important, but again Iran is not a country where power suits will make much difference. How you dress may depend on the people you are dealing with. Since the Islamic Revolution, the uniform of choice for state employees has been a suit with an open-necked shirt or a "granddad shirt" done up to the neck. No state employee would ever wear a tie, although, as we have seen, their popularity is picking up again in the private sector.

Presentations

Iranian business people also expect the highest standards in presentation and content from visiting foreign business people. It is probably best to start a presentation with some affable small talk, a little humor, and making sure everyone is comfortable. Eye contact and smiles are important, as is being seen as a human being rather than a robot. Humor is best made at your own expense—don't think for a moment about joking about Iran or Iranians, which can cause great offense. Some words in Persian will go a long way (*khosh amadid*! weclome!) and show you respect the society, as will expressing appreciation for the beauty of the the country and the hospitality of its people. Saying "*Iran kheli ghashang-e*" (Iran is very beautiful) will show you are not any old-in-and-out investor.

It is, of course, worth making a huge effort with the presentation. Given the high quality of education and knowledge in Iran, it will take a lot to impress them. Once the small talk is over, stack the presentation with facts and figures, clearly set out, to impress your hosts. Your Iranian interlocuteurs will likely smile and be unfailingly polite, but they may keep their true opinions to themselves initially, so you will only find out about the success (or otherwise) of your presentation later.

Negotiations

Diplomats involved in the marathon talks leading to the nuclear deal of 2015 in Vienna expressed exasperation and admiration over the Iranian negotiating strategy. The Iranians appeared to have limitless patience and were quite happy to spend hours or days negotiating on a fine point and then finding one small remaining issue once it seemed the accord had been reached. It is likely the negotiating style will be similar in business talks. There will be no hardball or macho tactics but it may be hard to work out what they really think behind the curtain of politeness. Bring patience, and a lot of it, to go over the details. An aggressive approach will not go down well; it is better to win respect by adopting the same softly-softly but very alert tactics of your hosts. Decisions are likely to be communicated afterward; a straight yes or no in the room right then would be out of keeping with the local culture.

Contracts

A contract once signed should be respected. Aim to
have bilingual versions in Persian and English. Use
English-speaking lawyers to carry out the necessary
checks. Trust or confidence (*etemaad*) is a very
important concept in Iranian society. All the small
talk referred to above is not just for the sake of it or
simply a cultural tradition; it is all part of the process
of building trust. A contract should be respected,
but as the country opens itself up to the outside
world it is worth keeping a wary eye on the political
winds, which could still change again at any time.
Risk factors, like a collapse of the nuclear accord or a
regional conflict, have to be taken into account. An
investment in the near future in Iran is always going to
be a risk but could also prove wildly successful.

Fulfillment

Disputes can be difficult and costly to resolve.
Becoming mired in the slow-moving Iranian legal
system is not something any foreign businessmen
would wish to be exposed to.

In the workplace itself, again the key word is
respect. Iranians of almost all political affiliations feel
their country was badly treated by the great empires
throughout the twentieth century and it's essential
not to be seen as a jumped-up twenty-first century
imperialist. Get to know people, their stories, show
an interest. It's fascinating and you will also win
their respect. Be scrupulously fair and never show
favoritism. Iranians of both genders can be feisty
workers and tempers can boil quite quickly. Iranian
employees appreciate strong, decisive, and fair
leadership. While being unfailingly polite, there may
also be moments when toughness is needed.

chapter nine

COMMUNICATING

THE PERSIAN LANGUAGE

The language of Iran is Persian (Farsi) and despite the existence of several important minority languages it is spoken by almost everyone in the country. For many foreigners, "Persian" conjures up the exotic and eastern. But, as we have seen, it belongs to the Indo-European family of languages—the same as most European languages like English, German, or French.

Modern Persian has its origins in the language spoken by the Indo-European Medean and Iranian tribes when they entered the area several thousand years ago. The preeminence of Persian began with Cyrus the Great and the Achaemenian dynasty. Iranians are still proud that their modern language goes back to this line of kings. It was written with the ancient wedge-shaped script of cuneiform and visitors to Iran can still admire trilingual writings in Old Persian, Babylonian, and Elamite stenciled at the ruins in the ancient capital of Persepolis. With the expansion of his realm, Darius I decreed that Aramaic should be the administrative language of the empire, but Persian was already cementing itself as the lingua franca of Iran.

The resilience of Persian in spite of centuries of linguistic invasions has been astonishing. The victory of Alexander the Great made Greek the official language of the realm under the Seleucid monarchs, a situation that was reversed when the Persian Sasanian kings came to power. But the biggest linguistic earthquake—one that still reverberates to this day—came in the seventh century with the Muslim conquest and the conversion to Islam; this ensured that Persian was written in the script of the language of the Prophet Mohammad and borrowed many of its words. To this day, Persian is written in the Arabic alphabet, with a few additional letters. Even more linguistic

turbulence came with the raids of the Turkic-speaking Mongols. The 1979 Islamic Revolution further accentuated the use of Arabic words and structures in Persian.

But despite these invasions, Persian has retained its distinct Indo-European identity to this day. First-time learners are normally struck by the similarities with European languages. Mother is *mader*, father is *pedar*, girl is *dokhtar*, water is *ab* (related to Latin "aqua"), and bad is simply *bad*. Grammatical structures are are familiar to speakers of European languages, for example conjugating the verb "to go" in the present tense brings familiar verb endings (*miravam, miravi, miravad, miravim, miravid, miravand*).

However, the situation is not all straightforward. As we have seen, Persian is written in a lightly adapted version of the Arabic alphabet and is read from right to left. The alphabet is tricky, given that the characters change their shape depending on whether they are at the beginning, middle, or end of a word; the vowels are often not indicated, leaving just the consonants. While Persian's Indo-European origins are still evident, Arabic has left its mark with its distinctive structures and large vocabulary.

COMMUNICATING IN EVERYDAY LIFE
Finding English Speakers

Very basic communication in Iran is not too difficult but expressing more complex ideas may require considerable language training. Most people in Iran do not speak English, although in a country with such high educational standards you will find many city dwellers who do.

Don't be surprised if an assertive woman—even one who is conservatively dressed—comes bounding up to you to show off her fluent English or French. Given the lack of opportunities available to practice their language skills, English speakers will often find visitors rather than the other way around. Generally the further away you are from a major city, the less chance you have of finding an English speaker. But in Iran, more than anywhere else, the unexpected is always possible.

Helpfully, all signs on major highways are written in Persian and English. Road signs in Tehran are also normally bilingual, frequent, and reliable. Outside the more touristy areas, you are very unlikely to find a menu in English, so you will have to ask the waiter what is available.

Speaking Persian

Mastering some basic words and phrases (see pages 79–80) will ensure instant popularity. Iranians are immensely proud of their language and how it has retained its difference from Arabic, which is even less widely spoken than English outside the clerical elite. The language also boasts a great literature, most famously in the work of the sensual medieval poets Hafez and Saadi but also in modern novels and poetry. Poetry is still important in daily life; it is not unusual to be stuck in a Tehran traffic jam and find the taxi driver suddenly reciting the verses of Hafez. Imagine being in London traffic and the driver suddenly waxing lyrical over a Shakespeare sonnet!

Persian Outside Iran

Iran is not the only country where Persian is spoken—it is the lingua franca of neighboring Afghanistan, where the dialect is known as Dari and is spoken by educated people of whatever ethnicity. Dari is intelligible to Persian speakers but strong accents and different words can make this difficult for outsiders. Persian is also the official language of the former Soviet republic of Tajikistan, where it is known as Tajik and is written in the Russian Cyrillic script. In both cases, the language is likely to have been spread by Persian-speaking soldiers forming the backbone of the armies that brought Islam to these countries in the later Arab invasions. Persian was also chosen as the court language of India under the Turkic Mughals, a situation that lasted right until British colonization.

GESTURES

Gestures are important to Iranians and many people wave their hands animatedly when in a conversation or an argument. But in this ultra-polite society there are a number of set gestures, most notably ones that imply respect toward a conversation partner. If an Iranian touches both palms to the forehead, this is a sign of great respect toward the person with whom they are talking. One gesture to avoid is the Western thumbs-up sign: in Iran, it is an obscene gesture and loosely translates as "up yours."

HUMOR

Iranians revel in humor, be it the slapstick comedies broadcast on television or something more sophisticated. The growth of the Internet and mobile communications has also had an effect on humor and extremely subtle jokes, frequently about politics, transmitted by SMS or over Facebook or Twitter, have become enormously popular throughout the country. Iranians also enjoy making jokes about the various ethnic groups that make up the country, such as the Turkic population in the north. Even individual towns have acquired particular connotations—the city of Qazvin is said to be full of homosexuals, while the women of the northern town of Rasht have a reputation for being wayward.

THE MEDIA
State Television

Television broadcasting in Iran has been monopolized by state channels. The programming is consequently often uninspiring, although the state broadcaster has been taking steps to rectify this in recent years. There are eight state-run domestic TV channels that can usually be picked up in Iranian cities, including one for sports and young people, a twenty-four-hour news network, a local channel, and a Koran channel. The main channels show plenty of news and also footage of the Islamic Revolution, the war against Iraq, and religious services to inspire the faithful. Sports are well covered and soccer fans will be delighted to know that English Premiership and La Liga games as well as European matches are broadcast live.

Soap operas are wildly popular, especially over the fasting month of Ramazan, and are likely to form one of the main topics of conversation in Tehran cafés. They tend to last for a dozen episodes and feature actors and actresses who are genuine stars in the country. In recent years, soap dramas imported from Turkey and dubbed into Persian have also become a national obsession.

Satellite Television

No private channels exist in Iran. This does not prevent a number of foreign-based channels seeking to beam their signals into the country, much to the displeasure of the authorities who regard such broadcasts as anti-regime propaganda and seek to block the signals. The most prominent such channel is the Persian service of the Voice of America, while Radio Free Europe/Liberty also has a Persian-language radio station known as Radio Farda. The BBC now has a Persian-language television channel that broadcasts from London and is detested by many Iranian officials for an alleged anti-Islamic Republic stance, but has won a wide following inside Iran and abroad. There are also many music channels pumping out the no-holds-barred Persian pop produced in Los Angeles and elsewhere.

In order to combat what they see as hostile broadcasting, the authorities have made satellite dishes illegal in Iran. They say the foreign-based Persian stations, as well as the other channels that can be picked up by satellite, risk polluting the public mind. Police periodically patrol neighborhoods and confiscate the illicit dishes lurking on the roofs of housing blocks. However, many flout the law all over the country and if their dish is confiscated merely put up another one. Strangely, it is possible to watch BBC World and CNN in most top-end hotels, including state-run ones.

State broadcasting (IRIB) also runs its own array of satellite channels for foreigners. Two channels show Iranian television programs to the outside world, often with subtitles. There is the slick and successful Al-Alam, an Arabic-language news channel that is popular with Shiites outside Iran. IRIB's Press-TV, launched in 2007, is an English-language satellite channel that broadcasts round-the-clock news combined with current affairs news documentaries. Its avowed aim is to break the Western stranglehold on the world's media by giving an Iran-based version of world events. Its journalism can be extremely slanted but the Web site has become much more informative in recent times as Iran cautiously opens up to the West.

Radio

The state radio channels offer a choice of traditional music, talk, sports, or religion. The most popular choices in Tehran at present appear to be Radio Javan (88.1 FM), which has surprisingly open discussions on many issues (listen in also for its hyperactive female presenters), and Radio Payam (107.7), which has music punctuated by news bulletins and all-important traffic information every fifteen minutes.

The Press

Despite state pressure and dozens of closures, the press in Iran remains one of the liveliest in the Middle East. The reformist liberal press had its heyday in the early years of the Khatami presidency, but hardliners subsequently closed down dozens of papers and even arrested journalists. There have been further closures in recent years and pressure from the state continues, but this has not stopped papers relaunching under a different name or new publications emerging. The liberal Iranian papers contain impressively learned articles about the latest films, international affairs, or scientific

 trends. They are also not afraid to criticize the government, especially on the economy, and the comments can on occasion be quite cutting. The finest reformist daily currently available is *Etemaad* (Confidence), which contains fine writing about international politics and Iranian society and has bounced back despite repeated bans. At the other end of the spectrum are the hardline papers that stress their loyalty to the Revolution and hostility to Western governments in every column inch. The best-known is the fiercely ideological *Kayhan* (Universe), whose editor is appointed by the Supreme Leader and whose editorials are required reading to understand what hardliners are thinking. English-language dailies include the *Tehran Times* and *Iran Daily*, but they are nowhere near as informative as the Persian-language newspapers. However, they do have the virtue of being easily obtainable at most Tehran newsstands. Buying Western newspapers or magazines is hard in Iran. Even if they are available (perhaps in a hotel shop), they are likely to be out-of-date, overpriced, and perhaps even lightly censored.

Internet Media
Iranians, especially in Tehran, now obtain news from online media as much as from newspapers. A huge array of Web sites caters for every taste and affiliation ranging from kaleme.org, a site close to Mir Hossein Moussavi, to Baztab, which is said to be close to elements in the Revolutionary Guards. IranWire is a fine Web site in English and Persian encouraging citizen journalism, while good articles about Iran, often by Iranian journalists working inside Iran, can be found on the English-language Web site devoted to the Middle East, Al-Monitor.

TELECOMMUNICATIONS
Internet
Internet access is not at all bad in Iran; several service providers offer broadband and there are a number of Internet cafés. But the state telecommunications authorities block Web sites deemed to be hostile to the country or bad for public morality. These include obvious ones like the Web sites of outlawed opposition groups or

previously banned newspapers, as well as some more mainstream Web sites. There are also sites that appear to be blocked despite apparently being innocuous.

Social Media

Several of Iran's top leaders have embraced social media. President Hassan Rouhani has a widely followed Twitter account in English and Farsi, as does his charismatic English-speaking

foreign minister Mohammad Javad Zarif. Even Supreme Leader Ayatollah Ali Khamenei has an official Twitter account, although quite who writes his tweets is something of a mystery.

Despite this official enthusiasm, Twitter and Facebook are blocked in the country to ordinary Iranians. If this seems a contradiction, it is because it is. The authorities took fright in 2009 when social media were widely used to mobilize people for anti-government protests for the first time in the country. However, many Iranians download Virtual Private Network (VPN) software to get round the ban as a matter of routine and use social media on a daily basis. The writing of Persian in Facebook in Latin letters with a sprinkling of catchy English words, has even given birth to a new Internet-based slang of Farsi dubbed "Finglish."

Telephone

It is easy to dial abroad direct from a hotel or private home, but you cannot do this from a public phone box. The cell phone network has improved greatly over recent years thanks to the emergence of a second operator competing with the state monopoly (previously making a single call could take several attempts), but telephoning may still require a little persistence.

MAIL

Postal services are reliable but sending letters and packages to the West can be a little slow. However, international courier services like DHL and TNT do have a presence in Tehran. For sending letters inside the city, many Iranians use a motorbike courier (*peyk*), which is quick and relatively inexpensive.

CONCLUSION

Visiting Iran is a full-scale assault on the senses and the intellect. The country's rich history—both pre- and post-Islam—is apparent both in people's behavior and the architectural heritage. The streets beat with the dynamism of a fast-changing society that has witnessed huge political, social, and demographic upheavals over the last half century. Iranian women are among the most opinionated and ambitious in the Middle East. Preconceptions about the country are exploded on every street corner. Social behavior is often very different from the West—but also surprisingly similar. The official hostile rhetoric toward the West contrasts with the extraordinary openness and hospitality of the people.

This book has attempted to be a guide to the contradictions, complexities, and delights of this extraordinary country that has been misunderstood by outsiders for far too long and is now showing, albeit very cautious, signs of opening up. Some Iranians say that they have given up trying to understand their own country—but that does not mean that outsiders should not try. Surprises and stimulation await anyone willing to visit Iran for the first time.

Further Reading

de Bellaigue, Christopher. *In the Rose Garden of Martyrs: A Memoir of Iran*. London: Harper Perennial, 2005.

Byron, Robert. *The Road to Oxiana*. London: Penguin, 2007.

Curtis, John. *Ancient Persia*. London: British Museum Press, 2000.

Digard, Jean-Pierre, and Bernard Hourcade and Yann Richard. *L'Iran au XXe siècle*. Paris: Fayard, 2007.

Ebadi, Shirin. *Iran Awakening*. London: Rider, 2007.

Farzad, Narguess. *Modern Persian*. London: Hodder Headline, 2004.

Firouz, Eskander. *The Complete Fauna of Iran*. London: I. B. Tauris, 2005.

Gheissari, Ali, and Vali Nasr, *Democracy in Iran. History and the Quest for Liberty*. Oxford: Oxford University Press, 2006.

Issa, Rose, and Sheila Whitaker (eds). *Life and Art. The New Iranian Cinema*. National Film Theatre/British Film Institute: London, 1999.

Keddie, Nikki R. *Modern Iran*. New Haven, Conn.: Yale, 2006.

Kinzer, Stephen. *All The Shah's Men*. Hoboken, N.J.: Wiley, 2003.

Mottahedeh, Roy. *The Mantle of the Prophet*. Oxford: One World, 2000.

Naipul, V. S. *Beyond Belief*. London: Little Brown, 1998.

Nasr, Vali. *The Shia Revival: How Conflicts Within Islam Will Shape the Future*. London: W. W. Norton, 2006.

Sadr, Hamid Reza. *Iranian Cinema, A Political History*. London: I. B. Tauris, 2006.

Shaida, Margaret. *The Legendary Cuisine of Persia*. London: Grub Street, 2000.

Thackston, Wheeler M. *An Introduction to Persian*. Bethsheda, Md.: Ibex, 1993.

Useful Web Sites

http://www.IranianVisa.com
Visa information and services for Iran

http://www.IranianTours.com
A variety of group and individual tours in Iran

http://www.IranHotelInfo.com
Iran hotel information and bookings

http://www.IranTravelInsurance.com
Iran travel insurance services

http://www.IranBC.com
Iran Business Centre

Index

Acknowledgment

This book is for my mum and dad, with love and gratitude.